VINUM

THE STORY OF ROMAN WINE

VINUM

THE STORY OF ROMAN WINE

STUART J. FLEMING

ART FLAIR

GLEN MILLS, PA

CREDITS
  Design Consultants
  Rock Hill Communications, Bala Cynwyd, Pa

LAYOUT AND PRINTING
  Piccari Press, Inc., Warminster, Pa

Copyright ©2001
Art Flair
P.O. Box 323
Glen Mills, Pa 19342-0323

Printed in the United States of America
ISBN 0-9712742-0-7

CONTENTS

ACKNOWLEDGMENTS

I wish to express my appreciation to the staff of various photographic services at sister institutions worldwide, who were so patient with my often unusual requests for artwork; particularly, to Irene Kohl of the Österreichische Nationalbibliothek, Janet Larkin and Tania Watkins of the British Museum, Guido Cornini of the Monumenti Musei e Gallerie Pontificie in the Vatican, Allen Patterson of Kew Gardens, and Jeremy Finlay of A-Z Botanical Collections.

Special thanks must go to Ralph Rosen, for his patient translation of the complex texts that are included in the Plates; Veronica Socha, for producing such superb line art; and to all those who have encouraged and/or cajoled me during this venture to ensure it came to fruition, among them Phyllis Katz, Gregory Maslow, Piero Mastroberardino, Sophie Socha, Charlene Sugihara, and Karen Vellucci.

CREDITS FOR PHOTOGRAPHS AND ARTWORK

*h=heading illustration for that chapter

Allen Paterson: Plates 30, 48, 55, and XVh

Andrea Jacobs: Plates IA, 3(inset), 6, 10, 12, 16, 42, and 70

Antikensammlung, Staatliche Museen, Berlin: Plates 36, 37, Ih, and Frontispiece

A–Z Botanical Collections, London: Plates 17, 46, 50, 51, 54, and IXh

Biblioteca Medicia Laurenziana, Florence: Plate XXh

Copyright British Museum: Plates 2, 7, 14, 39, 40,41, 47, 57, 61, 62, 66, 67, 68A, IIIh, VIh, and XVIh

CNRS-Centre Camille Jullian, Aix-en-Provence: Plate 3

Egypt Exploration Society, London: Plates 9, 15, and 22

English Heritage, London: Plate 5

Foto Roncaglia of Trieste, for Bilbiliotheque Estense de Modene: Plate XVIIIh

J. Paul Getty Museum, Malibu: Plate 73

La Bibilioteca Apostolica Vaticana, Vatican City: Plates Xh, and XXIh

Library of the Topkapi Museum. Istanbul: Plate 64

Lindsay Shafer: Plate 9(Inset)

Monumenti Musei e Gallerie Pontificie, Vatican City: Plates 19, 32, 34, 76, and Vh

Museé Calvet, Avignon: Plate 4(inset)

Musée du Louvre, Paris: Plate 18(inset)

Musee Romain Avenches: Foreword

Museum of London: Plate 5(inset)

National Gallery of Art, London: Plate XIVh

Österreichische Nationalbibliotek, Vienna: Plates 20, 35, 45, 53, 56, 75, and XVIIIh

Piero Mastroberardino: Plates 65, and VIIh

Provinciaal Museum G.M. Kam, Nijmegen: Plate VIIIh

Rheinisches Landesmuseum Trier: Plate IIh

Römermuseum, Augst: Plate 38

Soprintendenza acheologica della province di Napoli: Plates 44, and 72

Studium Biblicum Franciscanum Archive, Jerusalem: Plate 28(inset)

The British Library, London: Plate 71

University of Pennsylvania Museum, Philadelphia: Plate 6(inset), 8, 21, 25, 60, 68B(insets), IVh, XIh, and XIIh

Veronica Socha, Philadelphia: Plates 4A, 4B, IIB, IIC, 13, 23, 24, 26, 27, 28, 58, 59, 63, 68B, 69, XIIIh, and XIXh

Zachary Christman: Plates IB, IIA, 18, 43, and 74

FOREWORD

Then how could you know the whole from just the first taste? There are not the same, but always new things being said on new subjects, unlike wine, which is always the same. So, my friend, unless you drink the whole butt, your tipsiness has been of no purpose; god seems to me to have hidden the good of philosophy right down at the bottom, beneath the lees. (Lucian, *Concerning the Sects* LX: Lycinus to Hermotimus)

For the Romans, wine was something very special: it was a part of almost every aspect of their daily life. Along with grain and olive oil, it was the backbone of their economy, while private fortunes often hung upon whether or not an amphora-laden ship reached its destination. Wine made herbal medicines palatable and wound-poultices effective; it eased the path of business deals and brought laughter to the dinner table. Among the poverty-stricken, it made life simply more bearable.

The way that viticulture developed over time is a fine mirror of many of the major political and social changes which took place in the Roman World. In the late 1st century B.C., as fast-growing urban populations strained the agricultural resources of Italy, wine production in the Western provinces took up the slack and soon dominated the marketplace. When Septimius Severus took revenge upon those who had resisted his rise to power, the economies of the Spanish provinces were eclipsed, while the vintners of his native north Africa flourished. So it was in later centuries as well, revitalization of agriculture in the eastern provinces during the 4th century A.D. resulting in Palestinian wines being ranked of sufficient quality to be used in Christian Communion throughout the Empire. And whenever wars ravaged the land, or plague ravaged its people, Roman vineyards and their vintners had to fight for survival.

Individual attitudes about wine reflect strongly the social divisions within Roman society. The wealthy indulged in drinking sessions that emulated the Greek *symposion*, letting the flow of wine loosen the tongue and encourage philosophical debate, some of it weighty, some of it frivolous. Meanwhile the poorest of the Roman citizenry gathered in taverns, there to share the day's experiences and play raucous drinking games; conviviality usually gave way to drunkenness and mischief. As for the enslaved, they eked out what pleasure they could from a watery wine-cum-vinegar (*lora*) produced from the mash-like leftovers of the grape harvest's last pressing.

Predictably, Roman literature abounds with the familiar rival views about wine's merits—on the one hand, a social evil, the force for idleness and debauchery; on the other, a gift from the gods, a catalyst for friendship and a means to well-being. The pious and the alcoholic alike agreed, however, that wine was always safer for you than drinking from a city's disease-ridden water supply. Such disease kept life expectancy short, so the Romans expected much of life. Perhaps one particular epitaph captures their emotions most clearly:
"Baths, wine, and sex ruins our bodies. But what makes life worth while except baths, wine, and sex?"

Stuart Fleming
June 5th, 2001
www.romanwine.com

Here when Caesar has bidden the Roman chieftains and the ranks of knighthood recline together at a thousand tables, Ceres herself with robe upgirt and Bacchus strive to serve them. So bounteous were the gliding wheels of airy Triptolemus; so did Lyaeus ["the relaxer," meaning Bacchus] overshadow the bare hills and sober fields with branches of his vines.

(Statius, *Silvae* IV.ii)

Head of a bronze *Bacchus* found at Aventicum (modern Avenches) in Switzerland
2nd century A.D.

FROM VINE TO WINE

T HE EASE WITH WHICH THE JUICES OF THE GRAPE FERMENT NATURALLY INTO WINE belies the complexity of what is one of the most elegant chemical processes in Nature. Back in 1810, Joseph Gay-Lussac recognizied a key element of the process—the breakdown of the grape's sugar content into alcohol and carbon dioxide. But more than forty more years were to pass before Louis Pasteur identified the catalyst for that breakdown—microscopic organisms that we call yeast.

We now know that the skins of growing grapes are covered with a natural bloom, a waxy film that captures the cells of wind- and insect-borne molds and wild yeasts. The skin of a grape may have as many as 10 million yeast cells on it. Only a mere a hundreth or so of these cells are ones from yeasts that will stimulate the fermentation process that leads to wine, and of those yeasts by far the most active one is *Saccharomyces cerevisiae* var. *ellipsoideus*. It is the enzymes of wine yeasts that are responsible for the conversion of the grape's sugars to alcohol, and for the creation of the numerous by-products which partially account for the flavor of the wine (Amerine 1964). In some old European vineyards, the grapes and yeasts seem to have established a natural harmony that brings out the grapes' best qualities in the wine. (Such a notion of biological harmony reminds me of the kind of relationship which also seems to exist between the wort and local yeast strains that control the complex fermentation processes for some of the renowned beers of northern Europe, such as the lambics of the Payottenland valley to the west of Brussels in Belgium: see Keersmaecker [1996].) These days, however, most wineries, even in Europe, improve on nature by adding pure cultures to desirable yeasts and using chemicals to suppress the undesirable ones that also are present on the grape skins.

The grape is a complex product of soil and various aspects of climate, particularly temperature. A long growing season in cooler climes, such as the region around Bordeaux in France, yields grapes with a high acidity (Wagner 1974). Such acidity is an important factor in the development of the flavors that define quality among dry table wines. A warm climate, such as that of Andalucia region of southern Spain, ensures a good harvest of grapes with a high sugar content. These grapes lack the acidity and therefore the subtler constituents of their northern cousins, but they are well-suited to production of sweet dessert wines.

A grape is about 15% solids—skin, stem, and seeds—and about 85%, the pulp and juice that we call the *must*. Most of the must is water: its sugar content, as a mix of glucose and fructose, ranges between 18% and 25% by weight. Grapes used for table wines contain glucose and fructose in roughly equal amounts; those used for dessert wines have rather more fructose. Acids contribute about 0.3% to 1.5% to the grape's weight. The principal ones are tartaric acid and malic acid, but there are small amounts of other acids as well—citric and oxalic, among them each of which do influence the microchemistry of winemaking to some degree.

While these sugars and acids define a wine's main elements of flavor, many other constituents of the grape play a part in defining its subtler qualities, and thus the aroma and bouquet of the wine produced from it (Robinson 1999). Various amino acids, vitamins, enzymes, and minerals provide nutrients to the fermenting yeasts and thereafter become part of the process by which a wine develops its aromatics; tannins in the grape's skin provide the astringency that characterizes red wines which are fermented from a mash of the entire grape; and a dozen or so pigments (*anthocyanins*) give the wine its color. With good reason, Maynard Amerine has described wine as a chemical symphony, comprising not just ethyl alcohol but a host of other ingredients that, in their possible permutations for combination, result in so many different tasteful harmonies.

M.A. Amerine, 1964: "Wine," *Scientific American* 211.2, 2-12.
Keersmaecker, J. de, 1996: "The mystery of Lambic beer," *Scientific American* 275.2, 74-81.
Robinson, J., 1999: *The Oxford Companion to Wine*, 39 and 99 (New York: Oxford University).
Wagner, P., 1974: "Wines, grape vines and climate," *Scientific American* 230.6: 106-115.

A stem-footed cup (Ht., 4.9 inches) from the late 1st century B.C. Hildesheim Treasure
Its main frieze is decorated with an outdoor scene full of allusions to the wine-god Bacchus
and the Greek theater.

I have a jar of Alban wine over nine years
old; in my garden, Phyllis, is parsley for
weaving garlands; there is a goodly store of
ivy which, binding back your hair, sets off
its beauty. The house gleams with silver
vessels; the altar wreathed with sacred
leafage yearns to be sprinkled with the
blood of an offered lamb.

(Horace, *Odes* IV.xi)

Grotesque theater masks on a silver cup
from the Hildeshiem Treasure
Late 1st century A.D.

Baths, wine, and sex ruins our bodies. But
what makes life worth living except baths,
wine, and sex?

(An epitaph discovered in Rome: *CIL* VI.15258)

There are two liquids that are specially
agreeable to the human body, wine inside
and oil outside. . . .

(Pliny, *Natural History* XIV.150)

I

INTRODUCTION

ANYONE WHO DELVES EVEN BRIEFLY INTO
ROMAN LITERATURE CANNOT FAIL TO BE STRUCK by the intensity with
which the citizenry of the large cities of the Roman World sought out
the pleasures of life. It is true that every morning, from the crack-of-
dawn onwards, almost everyone, shopkeepers and craftsfolk, traders and
businessmen, would energetically pursue their daily work routine, so that every
forum, marketplace, and backstreet hummed with singularly unrelaxed activity.
Many an early afternoon, however, was given over first to the thrills of the Circus
or exercise at a public gymnasium—quieter folk might go to the theater for the
performance of a Greek comedy or stroll the greener parts of the city—while
the mid-afternoon was taken up with a visit to the public baths (*thermae*), where
people could gossip with the friends and business associates. In the early evening,
in the hour or so before dusk, they again would set aside thoughts of work and

settle down for *cena*, their only heavy meal of the day. That meal invariably was accompanied by the consumption of wine, its flavors and its effects often becoming a conversation theme in its own right. Experiences would be shared about the quality of certain vintages and the regions from which they came, and conversations might degenerate into the comic description of evenings of excess, all with a vocabulary that, for the most part, would be familiar to any modern wine connoisseur or drunkard today.

If we were to try to travel back in time and place ourselves at that dining table in say the 6th century A.D., how could we hope to contribute knowledgeably to the conversations flowing around us? First, learn Latin, of course; but Greek as well, so that we could cite accurately the views of the numerous ancient scholars that we will meet off-and-on throughout this book, Athenaeus of Naucratis and Plutarch of Chaeronea being preeminent among them. We also would need a least a layman's understanding as to how plump grapes on the vine somewhere in a rural part of the Empire had been transformed into the richly flavored drink just placed before us. To do that, we would have to look at how things were, economically and socially, several centuries further back again, in the time when the Roman State was still a Republic.

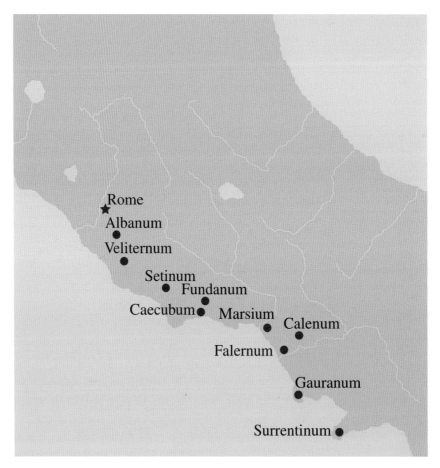

PLATE IA:

The most respected wines of the early 1st century A.D. were produced in the regions of Latium and Campania (Tchernia 1986). Even among these wines, however, there was a definite "pecking order" as to quality. For example, wine from Falernum ranked below that from Setinum and Caecubum but ahead of all the others marked here. Such views hinged on personal taste, of course. Pliny (*Natural History* XIV.64) noted the esteem in which wines from the Surrentinum area were held ". . .because of their thinness and health giving qualities," though the emperor Tiberius labeled them as "generous vinegar."

The Gauls filled themselves to repletion with wine and other luxuries, being intemperate in nature. . .Thus their bodies, being large and delicate and full of flabby flesh, grew by reason of excessive eating and drinking, heavy and corpulent, and quite incapable of running or hardship.

(Appian, *Roman History* IV.vii)

"The carting of wine barrels": detail from a stone relief at Trier 3rd century A.D.

II

MARKETS OLD AND NEW

THE SOILS OF THE ITALIAN COUNTRYSIDE OF THE EARLY 1ST CENTURY B.C. were fertile and fully able to nourish the peoples of the Italian Peninsula with all manner of produce, grapes included. The regions of Latium and Campania, which stretched southward from Rome and took in the rich farmland which curved around the Bay of Naples, then were producing ample amounts of very fine wine (Plate IA). From there came the vintages of Setinum that would particularly appeal to the palate of the emperor Augustus a few decades later; from there too came the vintages of Caecubum and Falernum that later poets and satirists recalled with particular fondness and not a little awe. At the same time, thoroughly respectable wines were being produced in several other regions on the Italian peninsula, among them Praetutium, which early on was spoken of highly by the Greeks; Picenum, which later exported much of its produce to the Celts beyond the Alps; and Tarentum, the produce of which the poet Horace reckoned one day just might rival the quality of Falernian (Plate IB).

Though the reputation of some Italian vineyards were definitely on the rise in these times, wealthier Romans still went to great expense to import certain Greek wines, such as Pramnian from around Smyrna (modern Izmir in northeastern Turkey) and Maronean from the eastern coastline of the Aegean Sea, both of which were mentioned in Homer's *The Odyssey*.[1] After all, it had been only a few decades earlier, in 121 B.C., when growing conditions apparently were near-ideal, that Italian farmers first produced a vintage of high stature—wines that all were identified as Opimian since that was the year of the consulship of

Lucius Opimius. Some of these wines are known to have been kept for almost two centuries, their value increasing more than twenty-fold, even though they had gradually reduced to the consistency of honey and had acquired a distinctly bitter flavor.[2]

During the half centuries either side of the Opimian year, a string of savagely fought wars and the skilful negotiation of alliance upon alliance slowly but surely had resulted in the toppling of each of Rome's competitors for power in the lands surrounding the Mediterranean. Thereafter, howev-er, the speed of expansion of Rome's territories was quite extraordinary. The thrust eastward of Pompey in 67 B.C.—initially a response to rampant piracy that had come close to blockading the ports through which grain and other essentials flowed to Rome—led to a four-year campaign that over-whelmed all of Anatolia and Syria and culminated in the capture of Jerusalem.

Scarcely a decade later, it was the turn of Julius Caesar to display Rome's military prowess (Plate 2). In 58 B.C., he brought to heel all the tribes of Gaul

■ LATIUM and CAMPANIA   ● Other well-respected wine-producing regions

PLATE 1B:

Some of the most respected wine-growing areas of ancient Italy outside of the regions of Latium and Campania:
• Picenum, Praetutium, and Tarentum are discussed in the Main Text here.
• The merits of wines from the Sabinum area are discussed in Endnotes [30] and [34].
• Rhaeticum was the homeland for the Allobrogica vine that eventually ensured the success of Gallic wine-making in the Rhône valley (see IV: A Broader Picture; also Pliny, *Natural History* XIV.18 and 26).
• The wines of the Pucinum area were much favored by the emperor Augustus' wife, Livia, who credited her long life of 83 years to their medicinal properties (see Pliny, *Natural History* XIV.60).
• The sweet, light wines of the Mamertinum area of Sicily gained recognition by virtue of being mentioned so often in Julius Caesar's correspondence (see Pliny, *Natural History* XIV.66).

PLATE 2:

Gold coin (*aureus*) depicting Julius Caesar (dictator, 48–44 B.C.) Interest in, and acceptance of the wines of Campania seems to have gained much from Falernian being served alongside the already famed Greek wine from Chios at a banquet in 60 B.C. that honored Julius Caesar's conquest of Spain (see Pliny, *Natural History* XIV.97).

and established a frontier along the course of the Rhine that was to survive for more than four centuries thereafter. In A.D. 46, he added the fertile coastline of Numidia (modern northeastern Algeria) to Rome's possessions in Africa. In all these areas, veterans of the military campaigns were rewarded with tracts of land or provided with homes in newly created urban colonies that were placed strategically to discourage any native rebellion.

So much wine was being produced on the Italian mainland throughout this late Republican period that the Romans were able to export large quantities of it to their new northwestern provinces. Ships laden with hundreds of wine-filled amphorae would ply their way along the Italian coastline from the Bay of Naples to the Gulf of Genoa and offload portions of their cargo at various ports between Genua and Narbo (modern Genoa and Narbonne, respectively) (Plates 3 and 4).[3] Cartloads of amphorae would be trundled inland to one of the many fast-expanding Gallic market-towns and cities of the day, there to provision the legions on active duty or to be sold to Roman war veterans who had settled close to where they had served. The rest went to the local Celtic leaders who by then had become little more than Rome's tax collectors. Of the latter, one historian wrote, with distaste:

> Being inordinately fond of wine, they gulp down what the merchants bring them quite undiluted. They have a furious passion for drink and get altogether beyond themselves, becoming so drunk that they fall asleep or lose their wits. (Diodorus Siculus, *History of the World* V.2) [4]

The Celtic passion for wine stemmed from the fact that it was a prestige commodity—a sign of wealth ranking alongside gold and thus an instrument of power. Gifts of wine to dependent relatives recalls the baskets of food that wealthier Romans might provide their business clients in times of need; and the provision of wine for the native poor at Celtic festivals went some way to ensuring political advancement. The stockpiling of wine conferred social stature; independent-minded Celts would travel to market towns such as Divona (modern Cahors) and arrange for the wine to be decanted out of Roman amphorae and into their own wooden barrels.

Roman traders took full advantage of the Celtic emotional demand for Italian wine in a variety of ways. They could barter just one amphora of it for the freedom of a poor native tribesman, at a time when the asking price for a slave in Rome was about sixty times higher. (Such deals provided the Italians with close to 15,000 slaves each year.) Alternatively, particularly in the mineral-rich regions of southwestern Gaul, they could seek exchange for the locally mined ores of silver, copper, and lead, or for some of the agricultural ironmongery for which the Celts justifiability were renowned. There too they could barter for the woollen clothing and salted hams which always fetched a good price back in Rome's open markets. Whatever the nature of the transaction, it seems likely that as many as 40,000 amphorae of wine were being imported into Gaul every year for all but the last couple of decades of the 1st century B.C., with Roman business negotiators decidely in control of this trade's organization.

Lucrative export arrangements of this kind did

PLATE 3A:

Underwater view of part of the La Madrague de Giens wreck site The ship that came to grief at La Madrague de Giens (near Toulon in southern France) was carrying fine wine from Pompeii to Marseille. The cargo of some 7000 amphorae of Caecubian wine (weighing about 350 U.S. tons) was a large one for its time (circa 60 B.C.); a third of that was more typical (Liou and Pomey 1985; Parker 1992). Today, the shapes of the amphorae, and the order in which they were stacked in the ship's hold, often are a valuable indicator of the ship's ports-of-call before it was wrecked. The loss of one of these ships to a storm or to piracy could bankrupt the businessmen who invested in its safe arrival in Gaul.

PLATE 3B:

Excavation of dockside contexts in Marseille have shown that the rise in the representation of Italic versus locally made amphorae was remarkably rapid. It took barely a century for their relative significance to be reversed (Goudineau 1983; Tchernia 1983).

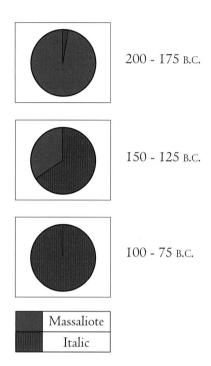

200 - 175 B.C.

150 - 125 B.C.

100 - 75 B.C.

| Massaliote |
| Italic |

not last, however. Rome's first emperor, Augustus (27 B.C.–A.D. 14), was very successful at turning the Italian mainland into a vibrant industrial world, satisfying the everyday needs of his subjects by the mass production of pottery, textiles, and glass. Well-administered seaborne trade across the breadth of the Empire also ensured the constant inflow of the domestic staples—grain, olive oil, papyrus, etc.—along with a lot of exotic items from the East, such as silks and the finest of perfume ingredients. But that success came at a cost. As dispossessed Italian peasants and wide-eyed provincials flocked towards Rome in search of work and a higher standard of living, the population of Italy's cities soared, and much of the surrounding farmland became pressed to provide sufficient produce for the local populace, let alone have a surplus for export. Many a vintner began to plant vines that offered a high yield of grapes rather than ones with a prestigious flavor.

Meanwhile, the output of the mines of Gaul was beginning to falter. The running of those which still could be made profitable was taken out of the hands of the locals and placed under imperial management. The earlier aggressive exchange of Italian wine for Gallic metals became less and less necessary. The Gauls now turned to the wine-growing districts closest to them, in northern Spain; and, since hardier varieties of vine now were being cultivated both there and in northern Italy, viticulture steadily moved northward.[5] Wine production in Gaul itself rose dramatically, so that by the time of the emperor Nero (A.D. 54–68) the direction of the Italian-Gallic wine trade was in full reverse.

Wine shops, like the ones recently excavated at Pompeii and Herculaneum, might include in their list as many Gallic wines as local Campanian ones, some of them priced quite low despite the great distance the foreign ones had traveled. By then,

PLATE 4A:

This type of amphora was *the* standard bulk wine container in the western part of the Roman World for almost a century after its first appearance around 130 B.C. Kiln sites for its production were concentrated in the Caecuban and Falernian Plains though some were produced north of Rome as well. It was standardized reasonably well to a capacity of about 48 *sextarii* [6.84 U.S. gallons or 25.9 liters].

It was mimicked subsequently in many other parts of the Roman World, particularly in coastal plain in northeastern Spain between Tarraco and Barcino (modern Tarragona and Barcelona, respectively). Working against the amphora's later use, however, was its own weight of about 55 U.S. pounds. The amphorae that eventually replaced it were either far larger and/or thinner-walled:

Type of amphora*	Weight of vessel average, U.S. lbs.	Weight of wine contents average, U.S. lbs
Dressel 2	33.0	55.2
Dressel 20	62.6	138
Africana Grande	39.3	137
Tripolitanian	34.8	122

* Data adapted from Peacock and Williams (1986: Table 1): see this source also, for illustrations of each of these amphora types.

A high wine-weight to amphora-weight will have made an appreciable difference to a cargo's value. A one-ton load comprising 25 full Dressel 2 amphorae would contain 166 U.S. gallons of wine, while a one ton load comprising just 14 full Tripolitanian amphorae would contain 209 U.S. gallons of wine.

Dressel IA amphora

PLATE 4B:

This type of amphora was produced predominantly in the Languedoc plain of southern Gaul around the mouth of the Rhône. It was particularly light, weighing only about a third of a Dressel 20 type. But the thinness of this amphora's walls may well have required straw packing to protect it during transportation (see INSET). It persisted from the mid 1st to the 3rd century A.D., generally being used to move wine northward across the Rhône-Rhine axis (Peacock and Williams 1986).

Gauloise 4 amphora

INSET

Stone relief depicting straw- or cord(?)-wrapped amphorae being hauled in a barge on a Gallic canal.

the prestigious Republican vineyards of Caecubum had fallen into disrepair; eventually they were destroyed with little compunction when Nero ordered construction of a canal from Lake Baiae to the port of Ostia.

This reversal was much criticized by writers of the day because of rampant hearsay that wines from southern Gaul—with the exception of those from the region of Massilia (modern Marseille)—somehow were colored artificially by smoke and sometimes were flavored with what, in terms of Roman taste at least, were noxious herbs such as aloe. But the tide of importation of provincial wines was not stemmed; indeed, popular demand required that it increase, and soon.

The Roman authorities did not despair. An underlying principle of early Roman expansion had been either to hold authority over primary cities at strategic points for foreign trade—for example, Alexandria and Palmyra in the East—or to occupy lands that directly could provide the State's leaders with luxuries and the general Roman citizenry with all domestic essentials. Early on in Roman history, Spain had fallen into this latter category—a youthful and debt-ridden Julius Caesar had plundered the western parts of it for gold and silver. Now Roman businessmen turned there attention to the southern Spanish province of Baetica. This was particularly lush and unexploited so that by the mid 1st century A.D. it was well on the way to becoming a vital source for Rome's domestic staples, such as grain and olive oil.

For the next century or so, it was Spanish rather than Italian wines that were being stocked in the warehouse cellars of the Mediterranean ports of Gaul. These same wines also moved by sea around the Atlantic coastline until they reached the southern ports of Roman Britain. Early in the 2nd century A.D., they moved still further north, to provision the storehouses of various forts and settlements that then were strung out across northern Britain (Plate 5).

PLATE 5:

Hadrian's Wall, looking east from Cuddy's Crag in northern England Our knowledge of long-range wine shipments to Roman Britain comes from interpretation of letters and symbols impressed upon the handles of hundreds of wine amphorae recovered from southern cities such as Londinium and Camulodunum (modern London and Colchester, respectively), and from the various forts along this Wall, such as Cilurnum and Corstopitum (modern Chesters and Corbridge, respectively).

INSET

The impression CANTONI.QVI on this amphora handle from Londinium is one of several shorthand variants on the name of the Spanish vintner, Gaius Antonius Quietus, who traded wine into the northwestern provinces extensively during the latter part of the 1st century A.D. His vineyards were located somewhere alongside the course of the river Baetis where it winds its way between Seville and Cordoba (Callender 1965).

Sardonyx cameo depicting the emperor Augustus
(reigned, 27 B.C.–A.D. 14)

And wherever one may go one finds the same story current—how one of the freedmen of his late emperor Augustus, who was the most skilful among them for his judgement and palate, in tasting wine for the emperor's table passed this remark to the master of the house where Augustus was visiting in regard to the wine of the district [in Spain]: 'the flavor of this wine is new to me, and it is not of a high class, but all the same I prophesy that the emperor will not drink any other'.

(Pliny, *Natural History* XIV.72)

III

WINE FOR ROME

ONLY A PART OF A CARGO COMING OUT OF SOUTHERN SPAIN'S VINEYARDS would be traded into the Gallic provinces—much of it was destined for Rome via the port of Ostia. There the amphorae-laden ships would share harbor protection with the massive grain carriers from Egypt and north Africa. Once the ship was secured at the quayside, its deck would become a hive of activity. Amphora carriers (*phalangarii*) would move up and down the gangplanks; other porters would empty the holds of their secondary cargoes, which might comprise sacks of nuts and crates of pottery and glass tableware; divers would salvage anything that dropped overboard. Several smaller boats would be moored nearby. These too would be busy spots, as dozens of amphorae from various ships were packed expertly together before being taken upstream to the mooring docks that lined the course of the Tiber in the southwestern corner of Rome (Plate 6). Once there, loads of amphorae would be delivered to wholesalers who would transfer their purchases into storage areas that they rented in nearby public warehouses, such as the Horrea Galbana.[6]

This storage would be temporary. Soon the amphorae would be carted onward to various cellars in Rome where the wine would be decanted into massive jars (*dolia*) that were sunk into the ground to keep them cool. (Locally produced wines presumably were stored in these cellars as well.) Wine most likely

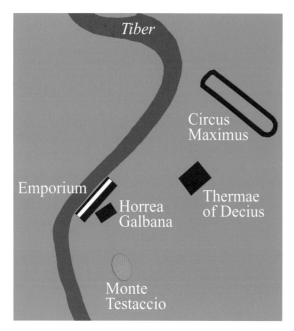

PLATE 6:

The Emporium complex on the eastern bank of the
Tiber river (after Rickman [1971])

INSET

The impression L.Q.S. marked the produce of a
Spanish vintner, Lucius Quintus Secundus [the
Elder], who exported wine both to Rome and to
the northwestern provinces, circa A.D. 80–130.
Fragments of his amphorae have been found as
far north as Hadrian's Wall (Callender 1965).

The Horrea Galbana was a whole palace
of commerce. By the time I had struggled
from the river wharf through the battling
crush of stevedores and porters who were
unloading barges and boats for the
Emporium I was in no mood to be lightly
impressed. It grated to enter this monstrous
establishment, built by a rich family as a
shortcut to even greater wealth. The rental
potential had always been enormous, even
though the Sulpicii Galbae were probably
unwilling to come down here themselves and
haggle over grain prices. They had been per-
sons of great status since Republican times;
one of them became Emperor. He only stuck
it for six months, but that must have been
long enough to bring the Granary under state
control.

(From Lindsey Davis' *Two for the Lions*)

was provided to the shops and taverns of the city in
somewhat smaller amphorae that could be loaded
onto hand-carts. Out on Rome's streets they would
jostle with pack-mules carrying the fresh farm produce from the surrounding countrysides.

Deep-layered bureaucracy was something that
had evolved insidiously within the Roman State
during its centuries-long expansion throughout the
Mediterranean region. So it was inevitable that the
several steps by which wine was traded over long
distances would attract volumes of official "paper-
work." Some of this took the form of painted
inscriptions (*tituli picti*) on the neck and shoulder of
the amphora itself. While wine production for
Rome was centered on the Italian peninsula, these

inscriptions were quite cursory. They became
increasingly detailed during the early 1st century
A.D., however, as Spanish provincial wines began to
dominate the marketplace.

There were usually three entries painted close
together, one above the other, on to the amphora's
body just below the neck. At the top would be
stated the empty weight of the amphora; in the
middle would be what is thought to be the name of
the retailing merchant (*mercator*); and at the bottom
would be stated the weight of the contents.
Over beside the handle, there might be a complex
group of symbols and words, including a crossed
R—an indication that the carrier's agent has
checked the content and value of the container—

then the name of the estate where the wine originated, the owner of that estate, and the name of whoever supervised the loading of the cargo. A consular date might be included here as well. Some amphorae bear a crudely scratched number that is thought to have some relevance to arrangement for storage in the horrea (see Plate 5, upper right). Early Byzantine amphorae bear a whole new set of such "labels," many of which demonstrate that Christianity had become the primary Roman religion by then (Plate 7).

Sadly, relatively few complete *tituli picti* have survived the passage of time. General in-use wear of the amphora's surface, or wet and acidic conditions during burial, have eroded away this thin layer of paintwork so that only scraps of this incredibly valuable information survives today. Nonetheless, the change in certain elements of these inscriptions mirror well the imperial confiscation of Spanish estates that occurred in the early 3rd century A.D.—more of this matter below—with the part of the *tituli picti* previously earmarked for the private merchant's name being replaced by an imperial formula, *Fisci rationalis provinciae Baeticae*. The name of the loading surpervisor was changed to a control mark for an imperial agent (*actores*) with such duties.

The chain of much smaller scale trade stretched onward every day, as household slaves, perhaps already laden with loaves of bread and vegetables, would come to a wine shop with some jugs and bottles in hand to replenish their owner's wine stocks (Plate 8). Tavern customers would be served their wine by the beaker with refills aplenty as long as there was sufficient coin around to pay

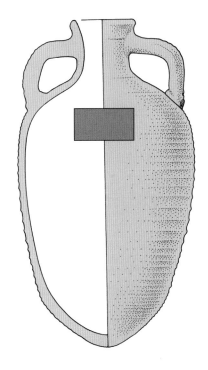

PLATE 7:

The *tituli picti* on this neck of an early Byzantine ribbed amphora is quite worn, but it is headed by the letters KMT ["Christ born of Mary"] followed by a monogrammed Cross. Below that, there is what appears to be a misspelt *oinos* [wine]. Other amphorae with this kind of inscription often have an additional Christian formula on them that translates "God's grace is a gain."

Though this amphora was found in Egypt, it most likely was made in, and traded from, the province of Cilicia (on the southern coast of Turkey). We cannot be sure, however, that the script was applied in connection with that trade. It may have been added later if, as was common practice in Egypt, the amphora were refilled (Geremek 1977).

PLATE 8:

This kind of glass bottle (Ht., 6.5 inches) with a capacity of about half a *sextarius*, was the common storage vessel for wine in a Roman household. Some wealthier folk might expect such jugs and bottles of wine to be delivered to them on a regular basis by hawkers who also worked the streets and marketplaces of the city in search of casual sales (Fleming 1999).
[1 *sextarius* = 1.14 U.S. pints or 0.54 liters]

the bill. The demand for wine in Rome during the 1st century A.D. was staggering—perhaps as much as *23 million* gallons a year (see Plate 41, INSET).

Each completed wholesale transaction resulted in the accumulation of dozens of empty amphorae near the riverfront. Some of them may have been used as ballast for the return boat trip to Ostia, there to join the amphorae emptied in Ostia itself for the sea voyage back to southern Spain. Huge numbers of them also were trashed over an area just south of the Horrea Galbana, year-in and year-out for almost a century and a half, from the early years of 2nd century A.D. onward, until they formed a mound (*Monte Testaccio*) that today stands some 150 feet high and half a mile around.

This mountain of waste is a fascinating time capsule of Roman history, particularly for the decades around the early 3rd century A.D. In its deeper levels, as we might expect from the above dis-cussion, Spanish amphorae are dominant. In its upper levels, however, north African amphorae first are mixed in with, then heavily outnumber, Spanish ones. The beginnings of the changeover coincides with the coming to power of Septimius Severus in A.D. 193. Among his first actions as emperor were to take revenge upon those who had resisted him in his rise to power. He executed dozens of politicians in Rome and turned his face *away* from the merchants of the Spanish provinces that had supported his rival, Albius Clodius. The emperor turned his face *towards* the north African town where he was born—Lepcis Magna (in modern Tripoli)—and encouraged a great deal of investment in the fertile farmlands which lay beyond it. Overall, the constantly changing content of the layers of Monte Testaccio sends us a message that would be echoed many times over: whoever was in power in Rome, for their own political safety, should always ensure the city's citizenry a due ration of wine as well as a full quota of bread.

Cone beaker with a distinctive eastern
Mediterranean "blue-blob" decoration
Late 3rd century A.D.

On account of their wealth the Persian kings
fell into such luxury that they sent for wheat
from Assus in Aeolis, for Chalymonian wine
from [Hebron in] Syria, and for water from
the Eulaeus, which is so far the lightest of all
waters. . . .

(Strabo, *Geography* XV.3)

IV

A BROADER PICTURE

SO MUCH OF ANCIENT ROMAN LITERA-
TURE—THE POEMS OF HORACE AND OVID, the technical treatises by
Cato and Varro that later were synthesized and extended by Pliny and
Columella, and so on (see XX: Sources, Ancient and Modern)—focused
on the fruitfulness of the countryside close to Rome. It gives the discussion of the wine trade in the Roman World a decidedly Italian bias. But logic of
scale dictates that, like Rome, many of the other great cities of the Empire, such
as the Egyptian port of Alexandria that most likely had a population of at least
half a million in the 1st century A.D., would have been importing appreciable
amounts of wine from afar to satisfy domestic demand.[7] At the same time, distribution patterns of amphorae fragments in archaeological contexts provide
ample evidence for all manner of province-to-province trade links which took
wine great distances across the sea and the land.

From the mid 1st through to the 3rd century A.D., the vintners of southern
Gaul exported a great deal of wine northward via the Rhône and Rhine rivers
(see Plate 4B). During the 3rd and 4th centuries A.D., Aegean wines moved as
far afield as southeastern Britain, the northern coastline of the Black Sea, and the
southern reaches of the Nile. An early 2nd century A.D. merchant's guide

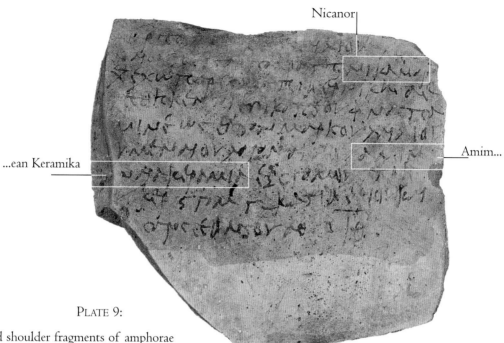

Nicanor

Amim...

...ean Keramika

PLATE 9:

Neck and shoulder fragments of amphorae
(*ostraca*) were used extensively in Egypt to document
trade transactions, details of which were scribbled in
shorthand Greek. This ostracon from the archives of
the firm of Nicanor at Koptos is a receipt for the safe
arrival of a shipment of six amphorae (*keramika*) of
Aminaean wine at the Red Sea port of Berenice (see
INSET). Whoever delivered the consignment to that
port on behalf of that firm had to present the receipt
to get paid for their work.

The Nicanor family was active at Koptos from at
least A.D. 6 to A.D. 62. They exported all manner of
goods to both Berenice and Myos Hormos—wheat and
wine mostly, but also rush-mats, drugs, clothing, silver
bullion, and even flowers. The Nicanor archives overall
indicate that they often acted as agents for the wealthy
Alexandrian family of Marcus Julius Alexander (Fuks
1951; Rathbone 1983).

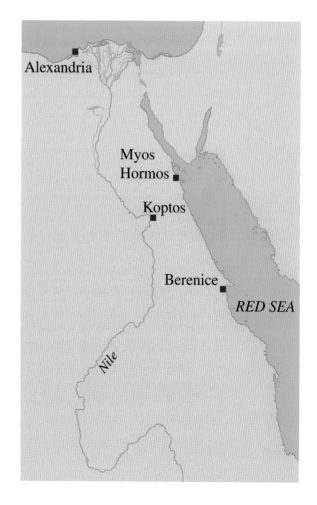

INSET MAP

These wines began their eastward travels in the massive
warehouses of Alexandria. From there they were shipped
up the Nile to Koptos (modern Qift), then across the
desert by camel to one of the Red Sea ports of Myos
Hormos or Berenice. Once out of the Red Sea, the line of
trade was either southward along the coast of Africa or
eastward as far as the tip of India, depending on the pre-
vailing trade wind (Casson 1979).

written in Greek—the so-called *Periplus Maris Erithraei*—records the shipment of wine (chiefly Italian, but also some Syrian) not just to the enclaves of merchants and their agents who carried out Rome's business in foreign lands (Plate 9) but also to places far beyond the Empire's frontiers, such as Barygaza (modern Broach) in northwestern India.

Over the centuries, there were a number of quite dramatic changes in the dynamics of the Roman wine trade. During the reigns of the emperors Hadrian and Antoninus Pius (A.D. 117–161), the Roman World certainly prospered—the internal strife over imperial power was far less than during the murderous reigns of Caligula and Nero during the mid 1st century A.D.; and the infrastructure of Roman trade by both land and sea was in particularly good shape in those times. There is ample material evidence that while so much of the Empire was experiencing an economic boom, however, things were going seriously wrong in central western Italy. Fine country villas that, in the heyday of their estates during the late 1st century A.D. could boast of near industrial-quality installations for the production of pottery, glassware, olive oil, and wine were falling into disrepair by about A.D. 170.[8]

We may never know for sure what so insidiously undermined the agricultural economy of the Italian peninsula at that time. Was the Italian soil truly close to exhaustion or was the infrastructure for land investment out of kilter in some way? Whatever the problem was, we can be sure that events for the next century and a half made putting things to rights too much of a challenge for the usually dogged Italian farmer. The plague that struck Rome in A.D. 167 and raged through the Empire for at least another fifteen years certainly took its toll on the rural workforce. So too did the regional conscription of farmhands that went hand-in-hand with the fifty years of civil war which ensued in A.D. 211 after the death of Septimius Severus. In the aftermath of these upheavals, Campanian vintages played only a minor role in the large-scale marketing of wine around the Mediterranean. Judging from the diverse origins of amphorae being off-

loaded at Ostia from the mid 3rd century A.D. onwards, Rome itself had to look much further afield than the farmland regions surrounding it to maintain an ample inflow of wines for its populace.

For a while, "further afield" certainly included the northern provinces of Gaul (Plate 10). The prolific Allobrogica vine that was native to its local woodlands had assured the eventual success of viticulture around Vienna (modern Vienne). The strategic importance of the nearby Roman veteran's colony of Lugdunum (modern Lyon) ensured that wines from this stretch of the Rhône valley went both northward to Rhineland frontiers and down river to the Mediterranean ports of southern Gaul and thence to Rome. By the mid 2nd century A.D., the traders of Lugdunum could draw on newly developed vineyards that had been established still further north, in the region around Augustodunum (modern Autun) that we now call the Côte d'Or. Right then, Gallic wine production was in very good shape indeed.

In about A.D. 170, as the plague spread westward, however, it is likely that the populations of the northwestern provinces were ravaged just as viciously as that of the Italian peninsula. Judging by the quality of decoration of many of its rural villas, however, Gaul's economy did recover remarkably well in the subsequent decades, seemingly because of a strong commercial link with the cities of Roman Britain.

A few decades later, fresh events brought about yet more economic decline in the Gallic provinces. They were not caught up so much in the imperial struggles in Rome, as in the vicious warfare that ensued when the forces of the Germanic confederation, known as the Alemanni, along with Frankish warbands, streamed across the Rhine frontier in A.D. 260. These invaders thrust southward as far as Tarraco (modern Tarragona) in northeastern Spain. At the same time, the Atlantic-bound regions became prey to pirate raids which steadily eroded the local economic structure. Eventually the main buildings on estates had to be abandoned as homes in favor of nearby bath-houses converted into rough-and-ready dwellings. As the network of trade in agricultural produce fell apart, an idled, and thus

PLATE 10:

Map of the Gallic provinces showing some of the main administrative cities and wine-growing regions during the 2nd century A.D. (after Cornell and Williams [1983])

At the time the older established vineyards of the Rhône valley were thriving so well, viticulture also was gaining a firm foothold in the wooded hinterland of the Gallic port-city of Burdigala (modern Bordeaux). Successful transplanting of the hardy Balisca vine of northern Spain enabled wine production in this region to become economically viable, despite the possibility of occasional cool, wet summers when the grapes might not fully ripen. Probably very little of this Burdigalan wine reached Rome though. This city was far better positioned to send its produce overseas to the wealthy Romans who were exploiting the tin resources of southwestern Britain and to the Irish court whose love of feasting matched that of the Gauls themselves (Johnson 1989).

disgruntled, peasantry finally lashed out in a series of slave uprisings during the 280s that undermined the Gallic economy even more.[9] If our more modern experiences with the American Revolutionary and Civil Wars are any indication, we can imagine how crops would have been foraged or trampled upon by roving bands of soldiers, both Roman and barbarian; farmers and their families would have ventured out in their fields only cautiously for fear of being murdered.

The Rhine frontier was restored repeatedly by the Romans and re-breached by fresh waves of bar-

PLATE 10, INSET

ROMAN	MODERN
Augusta Treverorum	Trier
Augusta Rauricurum	Augst
Augustodunum	Autun
Aventicum	Avenches
Burdigala	Bordeaux
Cenabum	Orleans
Colonia Agrippina	Cologne
Dibio	Dijon
Divona	Cahors
Limonum	Poitiers
Lugdunum	Lyon
Massilia	Marseille
Narbo	Narbonne
Novaesium	Neuss
Noviodunum	Nyons
Rotomagus	Rouen
Tolosa	Tolouse
Vienna	Vienne

The wealthiest city of Gaul was taken by storm no less than four times. . .the stench of the dead brought pestilence on the living; death breathed out death. . .What followed these calamities? The few men of rank who had survived the destruction demanded circuses from the emperor, as the sovereign remedy for a ruined city. (Salvianus, *On the Governance of God* VI.13)

So wrote the somewhat radical prebyster of Massilia who had witnessed the Frankish attack upon the city of Trier in A.D. 418. His comment captures the ongoing frustration felt in Rome about the inability of its provincial officials to maintain its Rhineland frontier, and the strong but by no means new, suspicion that their administration was corrupt and self-serving (see Plate 16). The officials in turn laid the blame at the feet of the Roman Senate; from the 3rd century A.D. on, the legions in the provinces were heavily loaded with barbarian merceneries whose allegiance was always in doubt. Salvianus viewed the Franks as an instrument of divine wrath against the decadent Empire, contrasting Christian laxity with the high morality of the barbarians who erred "in good faith."

barians. It was not until the turn of the 4th century A.D. that the successful campaigns of various generals, most of them family members of the emperor Diocletian, ensured that the major military crisis was over. By then however, as in Italy, the agricultural landscape of Gaul was in pretty poor shape. So it was that when the emperor Constantine visited Augustodunum in A.D. 312, he was told that the soil of the Côte d'Or was choked by a tangle of old vine roots, that the vines themselves were old and exhausted, and that the roads of the area were so potholed that wagons could bear scarcely half a load with safety. Though the real motive for this gloomy presentation of affairs was the hope for some tax relief, in truth it does seem that the vintners of the Rhône valley were no longer in a position to produce enough surplus wine to export anywhere, least of all to satisfy the ever-thirsty populace of Rome.

From this period on, vintners of the Eastern Mediterranean and northern Africa were able to pick up much of the slack for both Italy and Gaul (Plate 11). Let us remember that when Constantine became emperor in A.D. 307, he was embroiled in political conflict with the Senate in Rome and, in annoyed reaction, moved the administrative heart of the Empire to Constantinople. Within a few years of this city's founding in A.D. 324, it was bustling with administrators and craftsmen reminiscent of Augustan Rome three centuries earlier, and its people were as materialistic as anyone in the Western part of the Empire. Other Eastern Mediterranean cities, including Alexandria and Jerusalem, underwent appreciable urban revitalization as well. There was an upsurge of the economy of the Eastern provinces, from Asia Minor to Egypt, and wine production in the farmlands of those regions rose steadily during the subsequent two centuries.

In this period, the story of wine production in the Gaza region is particularly interesting. Like several others scattered throughout the coastal plains

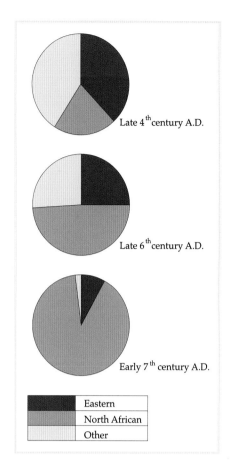

Late 4thcentury A.D.

Late 6thcentury A.D.

Early 7th century A.D.

	Eastern
	North African
	Other

PLATE IIA:

Excavations have shown that the representation of Eastern types among imported amphorae in dockside contexts at Massilia (modern Marseille) rose sharply during the late 4th/early 5th century A.D. Within two centuries, however, amphorae from north Africa became dominant (see Hitchner 1992).

Relative numbers do, however, somewhat skew information here about the amount of wine being imported: most of the Eastern amphorae types have significantly larger capacities than their north African counterparts (cf., the vessels in Plates IIb and IIc).

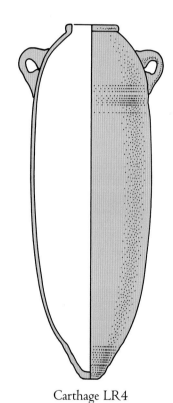

PLATE IIB:

Though certainly part of the trade that carried Palestinian wine from Gaza into the Gallic provinces, this type of amphora also appears in quantity at the port of Carthage in north Africa—hence its type designation—and in small numbers in the region of the Black Sea. Its form persisted from the 4th to the 6th century A.D. (Peacock and Williams 1986).

Carthage LR4

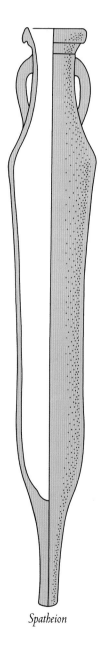

PLATE IIC:

This narrow-bodied amphora with a long tapering spike (*spathios*) appears in quantity at the port of Berenice (modern Benghazi) in the Cyrenaican province of north Africa. It had a wide distribution throughout the Mediterranean and into the Black Sea region from the late 4th to the 5th century A.D., with a smaller version being in circulation for the subsequent two centuries (Peacock and Williams 1986). Its capacity was about two-fifths that of the Carthage LR4 amphora type of Plate IIB.

Spatheion

Though certainly made somewhere on the Nile river in Egypt and found in large numbers at Alexandria, this amphora also occurs at sites in north Africa, particularly Carthage and Kellia (near modern Benghazi). Its type designation derives from the excavator of the latter (Egloff 1977). Its form persisted from the late 4th to the mid 6th century A.D. (Peacock and Williams 1986).

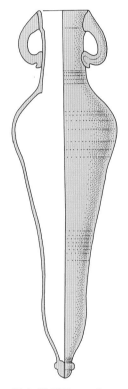

Egloff 172 amphora

PLATE 12:

Map of Rome's Eastern provinces (after Cornell and Williams [1983]) showing some of the primary cities and towns of the area, many of which also were renowned for the wine produced in the surrounding countryside (Broshi [1984], Mayerson [1985], Mayerson [1993], and Roll and Ayalon [1981]).

and low hillsides of the provinces of Judaea and Syria, it had been producing quality wine for centuries before the arrival of the Romans. As far as we can tell from the size and structural simplicity of the wine presses used in these earlier times, however, wine production levels were quite low and geared towards satisfying demand no more distant than the nearest major city.[10]

All that changed in the late 4th century A.D., as Roman society's mood was increasingly persuasive towards holy pilgrimage. More and more of the devout ventured forth along the centuries-old, but still well-maintained, network of roads and

sea routes that criss-crossed the Roman World. Constantinople, Jerusalem, and Mt. Sinai were the primary goals for such travelers heading eastward. But there were numerous well-tended shrines, such as that of St. John in Ephesus, which could be visited along the way. With stubborn determination for months on end, early pilgrims trudged the bandit-ridden roads and dirt tracks that linked Eastern towns to the myriad of monasteries and hallowed places where they had heard this or that particularly saintly relic could be found.[11] The ports of Gaza became the entry point for thousands of these pilgrims, and the

PLATE 14:

Gold coin (*solidus*) of Justin II (reigned, A.D. 565-578)

During the 6th century A.D., the heavy white wine of Gaza gained some favor at the Byzantine Court, as did a lighter variety from the vineyards of Ascalon just 12 miles further north along the Judaean coastline—thus this text from circa A.D. 566:

> Meanwhile the happy emperor with his holy wife [Justin II and the empress Sophia] had begun to partake of the blessed joys of the imperial table, the royal banquet and the sweet gifts of Bacchus, which wild Sarepta and Gaza had created, and which lovely Ascalon had given her happy colonists. . .and the draughts that the farmer had squeezed from the grapes of Methymna, fragrant, full of glassy Falernian. The ancient gifts of the Palestinian Lyaeus were mingled in, white with the color of snow and light with a bland taste. (Corippus, *In Praise of Emperor Justin* III.85: after Mayerson [1993])

Several Christian commentators indicate that Gazan wine was favored in the West for the sacrament (see Endnote 13).

ships that brought them could journey home with a valuable cargo of fine Palestinian wine that would sell extremely well in many parts of the Empire (Plate 12).[12]

From the 5th century A.D. onwards, an increased acceptance of Eastern Mediterranean wine in the West mirrors well the impact of fresh barbarian invasions that once again engulfed Rome's northwestern provinces (see Plate 10, INSET). The Germanic Vandals had swept across the Rhine frontier in A.D. 375 and cut a fiery and murderous swathe through Gaul, Spain, and northern Africa where, in A.D. 439, they settled in and around the port of Carthage. From there, well-organized piracy gave the Vandals near-complete control on the seas of the Western Mediterranean, so Rome lost the precious grain and oil that it had levied as taxes from its north African provinces for several centuries past. The cargoes of wine that now flowed easily into an affluent Carthage were predominantly Eastern in origin, including not only Gaza vintages but also those of Antioch in northwestern Syria and Sardis in western Asia Minor. Production levels in

Egypt were running at a sufficient surplus to satisfy both Alexandria's domestic needs and to allow for some exportation overseas, again to Carthage (Plate 13).

The dynamics of the wine trade changed again when, in A.D. 533, general Belisarius routed the Vandal forces of king Gelimar and so returned the rule of Carthage to the Byzantine emperor Justinian. The yoke of Roman authority and taxation was soon firmly back on the land, so heavier demands were put upon the African vineyards to create a consistent surplus. Thereafter, north African wines were traded without interference to the southeastern ports of Gaul where they found a solid market among the Franks. Palestinian wines gained some popularity in Egypt and Spain; they also were exported to Gaul where they ranked for taste alongside some of the still respected wines of Italy (Plate 14).[13] Rome's port of Ostia lay on some of the sea trading routes that linked the western bays of the Mediterranean, so the old capital could to some extent supplement the depleted wine resources of its own countryside with African and Palestinian vintages.

I built five ships, got a cargo of wine—
which was worth its weight in gold at the
time—and sent them to Rome. . .everyone
was wrecked, truth and no fairy tales.
Neptune gulped down thirty million
sestercii in one day. . . .

(Petronius, *Satyricon*.76)

You cannot have enough; for you get your
status from what you have.

(Horace, *Satires* I.61)

Marble bust of the Republican lawyer,
Marcus Tullius Cicero
(106–43 B.C.)

V

LEGIONS AND LEGALITIES

LMOST ALL THE TRADING PROCESSES
DISCUSSED THUS FAR WERE TWO-WAY ARRANGEMENTS, whether the wine
was sold either for cash or exchanged for other produce and materials.
Such was not the case, however, when it came to provisioning the army,
and the traffic in wine for the troops was surely appreciable. If soldiers
drank at least as much wine as the adult male citizens of Rome—each of which,
according to my estimates, was consuming a little short of 100 gallons per year
(see Plate 41, INSET)—then the consumption level of a five thousand-strong
legion on provincial duty during the late Republican era, for example, may have
been close to half a million gallons per year, perhaps far more.

To place such military procurement of wine in proper perspective within the
framework of the Roman wine trade overall, we should note that during the mid
1st century B.C., the Romans routinely maintained at least four legions in Gaul
and as many again in neighboring northern Spain, to discourage rebellion against
their authority. We also should remember that there was little native Gallic wine
production during that era; most of the wine supplied to those Roman legions
was shipped in from western Italy. To satisfy the needs of those legions would
have required the transfer of several hundred loads of amphorae every year. These
would have been transported on large cargo ships like the one which sank at La

Madrague de Giens, just twenty miles short of its presumed destination of Massilia (see Plate 3). This level of wine trafficking for the military most likely matched, and perhaps exceeded, the independently organized flow of wine to the provincial civilian population.

Of course, keeping the military well-provisioned with wine went beyond just good quartermastering. Life at the provincial frontiers was harsh and tense—in northwestern Europe it was bitterly cold and wet for half the year; in the East it was desert hot and dry almost year-round. During times of a civil war such as that which pitted Julius Caesar and Pompey against one another in 49 B.C. (when there were at least eleven active legions in Gaul alone) or during the periods when local tribes actively sought to disrupt Roman supply lines, soldiers would have been asked to stretch out their wine stocks, drinking it even if it was turning sour and only one stage short of being vinegar (*acetum*). At such times they might have recalled a grim era in the Spanish wars a hundred years earlier:

> Their soldiers were sick from watching and want of sleep, and because of the unaccustomed food which the country afforded. They had no wine, no salt, no vinegar, no oil, but lived on wheat and barley, and quantities of venison and rabbit's flesh boiled without salt, which caused dysentery, from which many died. (Appian, *The Wars of Spain* IX)

Political leaders, whether they were aspirants to senior positions in the Republic or emperors angling to retain the support of the armies which had brought them to power in the first place, realized that a long drawn out diet of *acetum*, however invigorating it might be, would soon turn the hearts and minds of the soldiery against them. The emperor Claudius, despite the stutteringly incompetent image that the modern historian Robert Graves presented of him in *I Claudius*, wisely pandered to his forces in Britain by passing on to them a tribute of fine wine extracted from the Rhodians of the Aegean. During the reign of the emperor Maurice in Constantinople (A.D. 582–602), generous rations of wine were provided troops that had been sent to

a town in Egypt to quell an outbreak of civilian violence (Plate 15).

Every single shipload of wine was a valuable commodity. The cargo of more than 7,000 wine amphorae on the merchantman that sank at La Madrague de Giens probably was worth about a quarter of a million *sestertii* as it was manhandled aboard at Ostia. (To put that value in perspective, a rank-and-file soldier then was earning less than 900 *sestertii* per year.) If an exchange for Celtic slaves eventually had taken place somewhere in southern Gaul, the value of the live cargo returned to Rome—assuming only two-thirds of the poor wretches would survive the journey—would be about 9 million *sestertii*. With wealth like that, you could buy a political appointment in Rome and position yourself well for yet more lucrative ventures of this kind.

Fortunes were made and lost quickly in the wine trade. The famous freedman Trimalchio of Petronius' *Satyricon* may have all but "lost his shirt" on one such venture (see this Section's heading), but a subsequent one, in which the cargo of wine was supplemented with bacon, beans, perfumes, and slaves, netted him a clear ten million *sestertii*. Though he used some of this money to purchase all the estates of his erstwhile master, subsequent loans that he made in and around the port of Puteoli (modern Pozzouli) made him wealthy beyond his wildest dreams.[14]

Such huge profits from the trading of wine, both military and civilian, inevitably attracted corruption.[15] During the early 1st century B.C., the Senate had to pass an edict called the *Lex Cornelia de Repetundis* which increased penalties on the ever-growing numbers of provincial governors being convicted for such activities. The need for Rome's foremost lawyer, Marcus Tullius Cicero, to defend someone as high-ranking as an ex-governor of Gaul, Marcus Fonteius, against corruption charges gives us some sense of how deeply rooted that problem was in the Roman governmental system (Plate 16).

We can be pretty sure that the network of merchants (*vinarii*) who were responsible for the procurement and distribution of such large quantities of wine were caught up in some of these scandals as

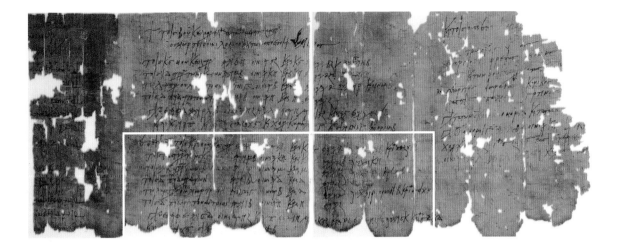

PLATE 15:

Part of a late 6th century A.D. papyrus from Oxyrhynchus, in middle Egypt
This part of the document itemizes in neat columns the amounts and costs of
bread, wine, meat, oil, and wood allocated to troops—among them Scythians
and mercenaries (*buccellarii*) drawn from various parts of the Empire—who had
been sent to restore order in a local town. The typical ration of wine (*oinos*) was
two *sextarii* per day (see Grenfell et al. [1924: P. Oxy. 2046])

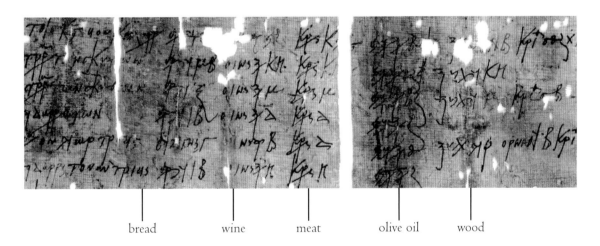

bread   wine   meat   olive oil   wood

well. Their clients' distrust of them led to questions about the quality of the wine that they were shipping hither and thither.

So low has our commercial honesty sank that only the names of the vintages are sold, the wines being adulturated as soon as they are poured into the vats. Accordingly, strange though it may seem, the more common the wine is today, the freer it is from impurities. (Pliny, *Natural History* XXIII.34)

There was something unique about wine that troubled Roman legal authorities for centuries—the fact that it could turn to vinegar during its storage and no one would be aware of that change. The vinegary odor and flavor of truly spoiled wine results from a secondary fermentation in the presence of special bacteria (*Mycoderma Aceti*) which grow by oxidizing the alcohol of the wine into acetic acid and ethyl acetate. The Romans recognized the endpoint of this chemistry well enough:

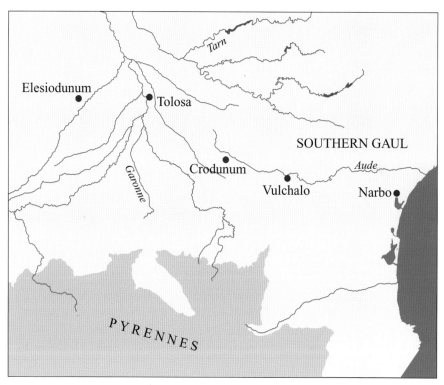

<figure>PLATE 16:</figure>

The crux of the charge of *crimen vinarius* laid against Marcus Fonteius was that, during the years 75–73 B.C., while he was governor (*praetor*) of Gallia—then only the region of Gaul south of the Alps—he arranged for a "transit tax" to be levied on each amphora of imported wine at various stages of its transportation inland from Narbo (modern Narbonne):

at Vulchalo (modern Carcassone), 2 *victoriati* [= 1 *denarius*];
at Crodunum (modern Castelnaudery), 3 *victoriati* [= 1.5 *denarii*]
and at Tolosa (moderne Toulouse), 4 *denarii*

These places were Roman garrisons. A merchant who diverted some of the wine through Elesiodunum (modern Montferran) to "the enemy"—most likely the Ruteni tribe—was taxed at 6 *denarii* per amphora.

The charge was grave since it alleged a taxation on Rome's own produce, and judging from the number of Gauls who bore witness against him, it is quite possible that Fonteius was guilty. The profits from such a venture would have been huge. But Cicero gained Fonteius' acquittal by unashamedly appealing to Roman prejudice against the Gauls, who traditionally were regarded as liars and drunkards (Middleton 1983).

It is a proof that wine is beginning to go bad if a sheet of lead, when dipped in it, turns a different color. (Pliny, *Natural History* XIV.130)

They called it *acor*, but they had no idea what caused it.[16]

Once the wine was ready to be stored, the Romans knew well enough how to keep their amphorae airtight. During the 1st century B.C., stoppers usually were made of cork wood (*Quercus suber*); in later centuries, preference shifted to a fired clay bung (*operculum*). Since neither of these provided a perfect seal, however, each would be smeared over with a heavy layer of lime-based mortar. So good Roman wine would stay that way, provided it was left alone. The trouble was that Roman vintners liked to meddle with wines, sometimes belatedly to add herbs for flavoring, but more often because they must have sensed/feared that *acor* was lurking out of their sight. The mystery was irresistible; stoppers repeatedly were cracked open, the state of the wine assessed and, whenever necessary, remedies were sought.

Whether he was writing from a background of

Scarlet-seeded iris (*Iris foetidissima*)

Fenugreek (*Trigonella foenum-graecum*)

PLATE 17A:

When mixed with a number of exotic oriental herbs, dried flower petals of this strongly scented plant were used to prepare *regale*, the "royal" unguent, so named because it was a special blend favored by the kings of Parthia during the 1st century A.D. (Pliny, *Natural History* XIII.18)

COLUMELLA'S RECIPE FOR A WINE PRESERVATIVE

> Crush an iris [root] which should be as white as possible and soak fenugreek in old wine, and then expose it to the sun or else put it in an oven to dry; then pound it up very small. . .Then into each vessel, which should contain seven *amphorae*, put an *uncium* and eight *scripula* of the preparation, and, if the must comes from marshy ground, three *heminae* of gypsum in each jar, or if it comes from newly established vineyards, a *sextarius*, or if it comes from old-established and dry places, one *hemina*. (Columella, *On Agriculture* XII.xxviii)

Quantities probably were quoted with care because the root-stock of iris is a strong purgative; or as Columella put it, "wholesome for the body."

[For modern equivalents of the various measures cited here, see XIX: Units of Capacity.]

PLATE 17B:

Dried leaves of this common herb, when mixed with catnip, marjoram, honey, and fresh olive oil, were used to prepare one of the most popular unguents of the 4th century B.C. (Pliny, *Natural History* XIII.13)

some bitter experiences, I don't know, but the 1st century A.D. agriculturalist, Lucius Columella, seems to have been particularly concerned about the problem.[17]

> From the time when you first put the covers on the wine jars until the spring equinox, it is enough to attend to the wine once every 36 days, and after the spring equinox twice in that period or, if the wine begins to 'flower' you will have to attend to it more ten, lest the 'flower' sinks to the bottom and ruin the the flavor. (Columella, *On Agriculture* XII.xxx)

If this "flowering" was the growth of strands of wild yeast that I think it is, then all the vintner's "attention"—whatever actions that entailed—was most likely doomed to failure.

Columella recommended addition of salt to the

must—that certainly will have beneficially increased the wine's acidity—and he suggested that storage amphorae be fumigated with rosemary or sweet bay [laurel], both of which have recognized antibacterial and antifungal properties. He added gypsum in a proportion of about 1-to-14 to a must that he felt was prone to turn acidic rather quickly; and he used a small amount of pitch resin, which also is well-known for its strong antibacterial action, to preserve wine after it had completed its second fermentation (see *On Agriculture* XII.xxiv-xxvii).[18] Elsewhere in his discussion of such matters, however, Columella put forward some scientifically much less sound ideas which appeared to argue that the battle for preservation could be won simply by pre-empting the onset of a sour odor with the sweet scent of some perfume ingredients (Plate 17).

Many cynical Romans suspected that the purpose of that kind of concoction was simply to disguise the onset of *acor* from unsuspecting buyers. Most likely they were right. At first, the destructive bacteria will form a near-invisible whitish film on the wine's surface and, as they multiply, cause the wine's volatile acidity to increase quite quickly. The wine is ruined long before the changeover to vinegar is at all obvious to anyone's sense of taste. The suggestion of various Roman jurists that a buyer should insist on sampling a batch of wine before signing off on its purchase, really offered protection only against outright fraud, i.e., when the seller knew full well that what was in the amphorae was already vinegar through and through. But the fact that the wine-to-vinegar degradation could occur silently during transportion and subsequent storage of what initially had seemed to be a quite satisfactory wine stock, left the legal aspects of these matters unresolved and contentious.[19]

Assuming that the vineyards are of the very worse sort, still, if taken care of, they will yield certainly one *culleus* of wine to the *iugerum*. . .But our own opinion is that vineyards that yield less than three *cullei* to the *iugerum* should be rooted out. . . .

(Columella, *On Agriculture* III.iii)

[I *culleus* = 20 amphorae = 137 U.S. gallons; and I *iugerum* = 0.62 acres]

"Lycurgus caught in Ambrosia's vine-tendrils": detail from the *Lycurgus Cup* 4th century A.D.

VI

THE VIRTUOUS VINE

AT FIRST SIGHT VITICULTURE—THE ACTUAL AGRI-CULTURAL ASPECT OF WINE'S PRODUCTION as opposed to its subsequent trade—would not seem to have been a wise business venture for a Roman to undertake. A new vineyard took several years to produce a crop and so demanded substantial initial capital investment, far more than either olive-growing or arable farming. Thereafter the maintenance of a vineyard was quite labor-intensive. Why would a man allow his wealth to be at the mercy of late Spring frosts and violent late Summer downpours, when as Trimalchio's eventual success had demonstrated, a dabbling in the trade of exotics such as Chinese silk and ivory, cinnamon bark and Oriental spices could ensure that he never had to work again? Why would he turn away from the long-standing Roman maxims, "Good is the smell of profits, wherever it comes from." (Juvenal, *The Satires* XIV.204), and "Seek money first; virtue after cash." (Horace, *Epistles* I.I)?

The answers seem to be many—some practical, some emotional. If a shipload of exotics was taken by pirates, how would one cope with the social disgrace of having to sell off one's property or becoming the brunt of a money lender's endless sneer? Conservatives such as Pliny always argued for a more prudent approach to the acquisition of wealth, and did believe that winemaking, in

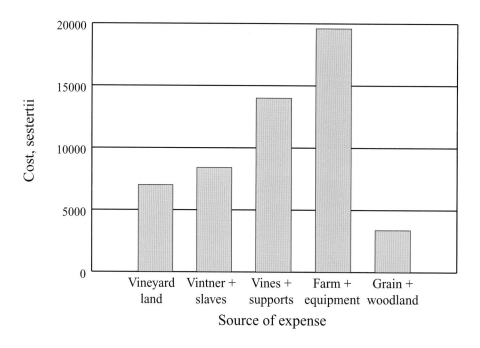

PLATE 18:

These costs of starting a vineyard are based in part upon figures used by Columella (*On Agriculture* III.iii), who reckoned that a vineyard of about 7 *iugera* (close to 4.4 acres) was about the limit of what could be managed practically by a single vinitor. But the capital outlay went far beyond just the obvious items—the vineyard's land, the vinitor, vine-cuttings and supporting trellises, and a slave labor force to put everything into place (Duncan-Jones 1982). Grape-crushing vats had to be built (see INSET); the vinitor and the slaves had to be housed and fed; various implements of wood and iron, such as ploughs and pruning hooks, had to be made or bought (see Varro, *On Agriculture* I.xxii); and farmland for grain and wood supplies had to be purchased and maintained. When all is said and done, however, these latter calculations are fraught with uncertainties; for example, whether the purchased farmland already had several usable buildings, whether there was a wine-press at hand that just needed renovation, and so on (Carandini 1983).

INSET

In the simplest Roman wine-press, a slave applied his whole weight to a pulley system that forced a heavy beam to squeeze down upon a wooden slab that was resting on top of a full sack of grapes. It's not at all certain what the other slave is doing in this scene from an early 3rd century A.D. mosaic at Saint-Roman-en-Gal in France. He seems to be trying to attach a rope to the bent-down lever. But ropes often were strung above the wine-press, so that treaders could keep their balance as the grapes beneath their feet were turned to mush (cf. the "torcular" wine-press shown in Plate 28, INSET).

the long term, could yield very substantial profits indeed. Columella, who owned several estates close to Rome, agreed with him.

It is true that, in Columella's time, someone starting from scratch and having to borrow the money to buy a suitably sized and reasonably fertile tract of land might face an upfront outlay of more than 52,000 *sestertii* (Plate 18). (A crucial decision at this point would be the choice of *vinitor*—a slave with proven capacity as a vine-dresser—whom Columella reckoned might cost as much as 8000 *sestertii*.) Then, for another six years or so, while the new vines were being tendered along towards their first major cropping season, he might be expected to spend about 2,600 *sestertii* per year to pay off his debt, feed and house his workforce, and maintain his buildings and equipment. So, by the time the vineyard was fully operational, the total investment could have been close to 68,000 *sestertii*.

To be marginally profitable, the entrepreneurial vintner needed his land to produce at least 35 amphorae of wine per acre on a regular basis—a reasonable expectation, allowing for some spoilage and judging from average yields of Italian vineyards today (see Endnote 68). Then he had to sell his wine at about 25 *sestertii* per amphora—again a reasonable expectation based upon the typical wholesale prices paid for decent quality wines by tavern-keepers in affluent cities such as Pompeii. If, however, the weather was kind and the *vinitor* skilled, far higher yields were possible—maybe three times above average (see this Section's heading)—and the venture's income would soar. A return on investment of more than 20% was quite possible, a figure that would put the vintner well ahead of the standard Roman interest rate of 6% that he could glean if he had opted instead to be a financier who loaned his money to others.

In low-yield years, it is true that there might be close to 0% profit.[20] But there also were several other ways to stretch the vineyard's profitability. The vintner's initial investment had to include some woodland of elm and poplar from which the stakes and props were cut that would support the vines. Vines planted in that woodland would soon wind their way upwards over the limbs of all the trees, and yield a valuable extra crop of grapes. Between the staked-out vines there was room to plant cuttings; according to Columella, as many as 26,000 of them per acre of vineyard. During the first years of the vineyard's life, these were reserve stocks that could replace vines which failed to mature in the vineyard itself, but cuttings subsequently taken from choice vines could become nursery plants. These were marketable in their own right just two years later. Their sale could yield a bonus of around 5,000 *sestertii* per acre of initial planting; an income which, in some years at least, might exceed that from the grape harvest itself.

The vintner, pondering on his investment, might well take a hard look at the cost of his slave labor as well. Columella was quite critical of many of his contemporaries who believed that any slave bought casually at a regular marketplace auction could be turned into a worthwhile *vinitor*. Still, several Roman literary sources indicated that other kinds of skilled slaves, such as a good cook, could be purchased in Rome for less than 3000 *sestertii*, so the 8000 *sestertii* spent by Columella on his vintner does appear rather exorbitant. As for the ancillary workforce, Columella and other landowners sometimes planned for the long-term by encouraging their slave women to have as many children as possible, even granting them their freedom when they bore more than three sons. A babe-in-arms one year would be a nimble-limbed grape-picker just a decade or so later.[21]

There also was the possibility of having some of the cultivation of the land done by chained slaves—usually ex-criminals or estate slaves being punished for some disobedience—who could be bought for just a couple of hundred *sestertii*. But some Romans had trouble with the morality and doubtful economics of this practice. For example, Pliny imagined that the Earth itself—". . .whose cultivation is spoken of as worship. . . ."—would be pained and indignant were her soil to be turned by ". . . slaves with fettered ankles and by the hands of malefactors with branded faces." (*Natural History* XVIII.21); and he argued that a chain-gang's work was inevitably ". . .utterly bad, as is everything else done by desperate men." (*Natural History* XVIII.35). Every other kind of saving that anyone came up with, however small, was respected by Rome's landed gentry and surely mimicked to good effect.[22]

With regard to the rest of their equipment—
'the mute,' a term that includes baskets, *dolia*
(wine vats), and the like. . .nothing should be
bought which can be raised on the place or
made by the men on the farm. . . .

(Varro, *On Agriculture* I.xxii)

Even so happily is cinnamon mingled with
its nard, even so happily Massic wines [are
mixed] with Theseus' honeycombs. No more
apt is the joining of elms with tender vines,
nor does the lotus more love the waters or
the myrtle the shore.

(Martial, *Epigrams* IV.13)

Vineyards established at Pompeii by the
Mastroberardino Winery, with Mt. Vesuvius
in the background

VII

AN EMOTIONAL INVESTMENT

SUCH WAS THE BUSINESS OF ROMAN VITICULTURE
as best we can reconstruct its structure. In a purely clinical way, a modern
Western economist, while assuredly pointing out the risks inherent in
growing such a weather-sensitive crop and the financial implications of a
drop in wholesale prices in a year of glut, probably would accept the idea
that wine production was a reasonable thing to attempt. (On the plus side, that
economist might note, as several Roman agriculturalists did in their day, that
long-lasting crops, such as wine and honey, could be stockpiled for a future year
when prices might be high.) But there had to be motivations other than just profit that drove the Roman estate owner in this direction. If you were anywhere near
a large Italian city—particularly Rome, of course—you could do far better by
growing expensive fruits, such as peaches, or by raising plump birds as banquet
fare (Plate 19).

It makes me blush for the present generation, if we are willing to believe that people can be found to pay 4000 *sestertii* for a pair of pigeons. . . . (Columella, *On Agriculture* VIII.viii.10)

Roman mosaics frequently depict the bounty of the Italian countryside and the waters of the Mediterranean; but such foodstuffs were expensive for city dwellers (Duncan-Jones 1982). In the mid 1st century A.D., estate-owners on the outskirts of Rome found it profitable to raise pigeons and turtle-doves through the winter on a diet of wine-soaked bread, and farm-fattened thrushes could be sold at 12 *sestertii* a piece (Columella, *On Agriculture* VIII.vii-x). A fine red mullet could cost 8000 *sestertii* in the Roman market, and fine wines as much as 1000 *sestertii* per amphora (see Pliny, *Natural History* IX.67 and XIV.57, respectively). It was even worthwhile for farmers to raise geese in Gaul and drive them across the Alps and along the Italian highways into Rome (see Pliny, *Natural History* X.53).

To get a handle on the emotional force behind the Roman fascination with the vine itself, the writings of the likes of Columella and Pliny have to be read in a broader context than just raw figures about costs and yields. So much of their discussion of agriculture is about work ethic rather than profit, in what amounts to a harking-back to the Republic's very roots in the Italian countryside. Some poets waxed lyrical about such matters.

> When the time is ripe, let me plant the tender vines and the stout orchard trees with my own deft hands, a countryman indeed. Nor let hope disappoint me, but even vouchsafe the heaped-up corn and rich new wine to fill my vat. For I bend in worship wherever flowery garlands lie on deserted tree-stock in the fields. . . . (Tibullus, *Elegies* I: The Poet's Ideal)

Other writers were simply nostalgic for those rough-and-ready days before Rome became the economic powerhouse of the Mediterranean World, and the binding of a vine to tall trees of the Campanian countryside had a yearning significance in the Roman psyche.

> Happy is the man who, far away from business cares. . .works his ancestral acres with his oxen, from all money-lending free. . .he avoids the Forum and proud thresholds of more powerful citizens; and so he either weds his lofty poplar trees to well-grown vines. . .and cutting off useless branches with the pruning knife, engrafts more fruitful ones. . . ." (Horace, *Epodes* II: Country Joys)

Underlying all these words was a romantic notion akin to that held by some present-day Americans about many of their early presidents; that Rome's ancient heroes—among them Horatius Cocles who in 508 B.C. held off the Etruscans at the Janiculum bridge until it was scuttled into the Tiber—were sturdy farmers who lived frugally and ploughed their own land until such day as they might be called upon to serve a direly threatened Republic.

The early senators who headed the centuries-long lineage of many renowned families of Imperial Rome also were credited with being "hands-on" farmers. By the 1st century A.D., the cultivation of vines, along with the other two domestic staple crops—wheat and olives—was a way to find a rapport with those fabled Republicans and their traditional ideals. It didn't matter if the land was so poor that the vine warranted pruning only every other year, as long as the landowner was diligent in his efforts to cope. If, by that diligence, he managed to turn a meager plot into something approaching that of the finest vineyards and produced the quality of grape to match, then the Romans drooled with respect for his achievement.

The profits from these clod-to-cuvée transformations of the landscape could be enormous. A case in point is the story of the freedman, Remmius Palaemon of Vicetia, who around 50 B.C. spent 600,000 *sestertii* on a farm in the Nomentum region northeast of Rome:

> To the latter he gave great attention, keeping shops for the sale of ready made clothing and cultivating his fields with such care that it is common talk that a vine which he grafted himself yielded three hundred and sixty bunches of grapes. (Suetonius, *The Lives of Illustrious Men*: On Grammarians, xxiii)

Eight years later he sold his grape crop for 400,000 *sestertii* while it was still hanging on the vine; a couple of years later still, he sold the entire farm to Emperor Nero's tutor, Lucius Seneca, for an incredible 2.4 million *sestertii*—thus four times what he originally paid for it.

What else we know of Palaemon does him little credit, his blatant licentiousness leading even the emperor Tiberius to question his moral fitness to teach young men. In Roman eyes, however, this freedman's viticultural skills were a decided plus sign in Palaemon's column of life because it had been achieved by hard labor. In contrast, Republican-minded Romans frowned upon retailers who sought a mark-up beyond the norm of about 25%; and they criticized those wealthy landowners who put so little energy into maintenance of their farms that their carts would only be laden with produce when *leaving* Rome and heading towards their villa estates.

Everyone knew that Italian wine shipped far beyond the Empire's Eastern frontiers could be bartered into a priceless return cargo of Oriental exotics (Plate 20). But Roman traditionalists held firm about the fiscal soundness of viticulture, stressing the impropriety of investment in ventures that were so prone to the risk of piracy and shipwreck—thus:

> . . .the merchant obtains no more profit by rashly trespassing on the seas, nor by going as far as the coast of the Red Sea or of the Indian Ocean to seek merchandise, than is yielded by a diligently cultivated homestead. (Pliny, *Natural History* XIV.52)

Columella went one step further, railing against men who wasted their days and their money in ". . .hypocritical fawning [and] demeaning servility," as they tried to buy senatorial honors, when to his mind they could have been farming "in the old-fashioned way, even in imprudent fashion by those without previous instruction." (see *On Agriculture* I. preface).

These ideas resonate today as we watch the evolution of the Stock Market, now seemingly divided into an "old economy" based upon core industries and domestic retailers, and a "new economy" of software developers and entrepreneurial IPO-hungry .coms. Pliny and his circle would have favored the former, but the Trimalchios of his time without question would have accepted the volatility and riskiness of the latter in the hope of dazzling short-term profits.

These ideas also represent Roman philosophical extremes, between which, in practice, there lay a whole spectrum of practical attitudes. True, in 218 B.C. a law—the *plebiscitum Claudianum*—had been passed that forbade senators from owning massive freighters; true too that there was public outcry when Aemilius Lepidus built a breakwater on the shoreline near his vineyard-rich estate at Tarracina (modern Terracina, roughly midway

PLATE 20:

This papyrus (known as *P. Vindob G 40822*) documents the details of a loan taken out, pledging as security the specific goods—six parcels of cargo exported on the *Hermapollon*, probably anchored at Myos Hormos or Berenice (see Plate 9)—that will be purchased with the borrowed money. The surviving text described just three of the parcels—a cosmetic herb (Gangetic nard), ivory tusks, and lengths of fine fabrics—weighing close to 137 talents [7920 U.S. pounds] with a value that might have approached 3.2 million *sestertii*. The transaction overall was valued at close to 27 million *sestertii* (Casson 1990).

A typical merchant ship working out of a Red Sea port would have a capacity of about 11,000 talents, which might roughly translate to an outgoing cargo of about 3100 full wine amphorae. Assuming the cost per amphora in Italy was about 15 *sestertii*, and allowing that transport charges and various taxes along the way would match that figure, then investment in this venture would amount to a mere 97,000 *sestertii*.

Gangetic nard, 60 containers   45.0 talents

Ivory, sound condition   78.9 talents

Fabric, 50 lengths   13.2 talents

between Rome and Naples) just after he had been appointed as a magistrate for the Tiberside district where the Emporium was being constructed (see Plate 6). By the early 1st century B.C., however, Rome's senators had set up complex network of family members, clients, and business-only friends (*amicitia*) through which profits from wine production—or anything else, for that matter—could be channeled back to them for use in political growth and maintenance of an appropriate life-style.[23] Such a fiscal network passed muster as long as it satisfied a certain code of behavior.

> What truly matters is first that such wealth be properly acquired, through no base or contemptible form of gain; next, that it be increased by intelligence, industriousness, and thrift [*ratio, diligentia, et parsimonia*]. (Cicero, *On Duties* I.92)

By Pliny's day, however, a senator's involvement in the commercial process had to be quite blatant if it was to attract criticism for a lack of *dignitas*.

You will forgive me if I say I prefer glass: at least it doesn't smell. If it were not so breakable I should prefer it even to gold; as it is, it is so cheap.

(Petronius, *Satyricon.* 50)

He (the emperor Gallienus) always drank out of gold cups; he despised a glass, because nothing was more common, he said.

(Trebellius Pollio, *Augustan Histories:*
The Two Gallieni XVII.5)

Bronze wine vessels from various 4th century A.D. burials at Nijmegen, on the Rhine friontier.

VIII

JARS AND JUGS,
BOTTLES AND BEAKERS

THE VITAL ROLE THAT THE TRIAD OF GRAIN, WINE, AND OLIVE OIL PLAYED IN THE ROMAN ECONOMY permeates ancient literature of all kinds. I have cited a few instances of this already, but there are hundreds more, not least among them, the Old Testament texts that molded the views of the Jewish communities of Rome's Eastern Mediterranean provinces. One of God's greatest gifts was the promise of fertile lands.

He causes the grass to grow for the cattle, and the herb for the service of man; that he may bring forth food out of the earth, and wine that gladdens the heart of man, and oil to make his face shine, and bread that strengthens man's heart. (*Psalms* CIV.15)

By equal token, it was accepted as a sign of divine anger if these crops were lost.

The Lord will bring a nation against you from afar. . .who shall not leave you grain, wine, or oil, the increase in your cattle or the young of your flock, until they have caused you to perish. (*Deuteronomy* XXVIII.51)

It wasn't just farmers, however, who worried about such matters. The annual cycle for each of the crops involved many peripheral activities and livelihoods. Equipment such as mills and presses had to be built or repaired; wagons and boats had to be kept in good order. The craft most intimately related to wine production was amphora-making, so to some extent the potter's fortune swung back-and-forth with that of the vintner.

In the earlier part of the Republican era, farm tracts were quite small—the 2 *iugera* [about 1.2 acres] given to each of the 300 colonists at the coastal town of Tarracina Anxur (modern Terracina), when it was founded in 329 B.C. would have provided only a subsistence living. With some regional variations, such an allocation seems to have been typical for that time and for a century or so more thereafter.[24] That land can only have been committed partially to viticulture, so early vintners most likely pooled their wine yields each year at a few local cellars which in turn contracted with a local pottery workshop for storage and transport amphorae. Such farmers, as property owners, however, were eligible for military service. Over the centuries-long period of Rome's territorial expansion, many land plots were tended poorly for years on end. Subsistence farmers were forced to sell and migrate to the cities in search of work. Despite a land reform introduced by the tribune Tiberius Sempronius Gracchus in 133 B.C., the Italian landscape gradually transformed into a socially divided patchwork of estates at prime locations that were owned by just a few Roman families, and a myriad of remote, less fertile plots where peasants eked out a wretched life on the edge of starvation. Many of those peasants eventually came cap-in-hand to the patrician farm owners, seeking to labor for a pittance alongside the estate's slaves in the vineyards and hay-fields.

What happened at Cosa (near modern Orbetello) is particularly relevant to our story. When that port town was founded in 273 B.C., each colonist was given a paltry 6 *iugera*. By the turn of the 2nd century B.C., however, there were at least a dozen fine villas scattered through the surrounding countryside, each with estates of 500 *iugera* or more. One of these estates was owned by a senatorial family, the Sestii, whose exportation of wine to Gaul is dramatically highlighted by the hundreds of amphora necks stamped SES recently recovered from the Grande Conglué shipwreck just offshore from Marseille. Dozens of similarly marked fragments found around Cosa's ancient harbor indicate that the Sestius estate produced its own amphorae, presumably in numbers that depended each year on the wine-yield of their vineyards.

Such a cost-effective organization of estate activities was by no means unique in its day. Amphorae bearing estate markings of one of Julius Caesar's buisiness associates, Rabirius Postumus, have been found in Germany and Sicily. Those of Cicero's friend, Marcus Tuccius Galeo, whose estate was near Brundisium (modern Brindisi), have been

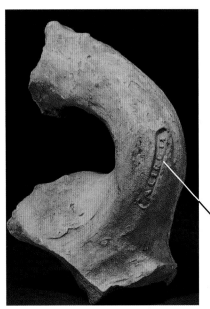

PLATE 21:

The impression ACIRGI on this amphora handle from Monte Testaccio is thought to represent a vintner who was active in southern Spain circa A.D. 90–140. Variants on this impression often include shorthand versions of the word *figlina* ("pottery"), which would suggest that the owner of the estate Acirgiana took the commercially wise step of producing not only a fine wine but also the amphorae in which it could be transported to foreign lands (Callender 1965). Another quite common variant, ACIR-GI//M.S. MAVRI, may indicate an expansion of the activities of the *figlina Acirgiana* to include provision of amphorae for a new estate owned by a certain M.S. Maurianus.

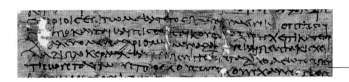

TRANSLATION

I make for you, fire, refire and coat with pitch what are
termed Oxyrhynchite four-*choes* jars to the number of
15,000, 150 double *keramica* [= eight-*choes* jars] and 150
two-*choes* jar . . . .
[I *chous* is estimated to be about 1.27 U.S. gallons
or 4.85 liters]

PLATE 22:

Part of the Oxyrhynchus papyrus 3595, dated A.D. 243
The deal struck in this lease has the owner of an estate near the village of Senepta providing a workshop, complete with store-rooms, a
potter's wheel, and a supply of suitable clays, fuel for the kiln, and a
stock of pitch sealant, while the potter (Aurelius Paesis) would bring
with him sufficient craftsmen and stokers to complete the job on
time (Cockle 1981).
Assuming the largest and smallest jars were not used for long-term
storage, the 15,000 four-*choes* jars would have been used to keep
and/or ship close to 77,000 U.S. gallons of wine.

recovered from the Planier shipwreck, again offshore
from Marseille. During the latter part of the 1st
century A.D., landowners of southern Spain came to
dominate trade in the Western Empire, not just of
wine but olive oil and the fish sauce *garum* as well.
Their estates also would include an amphora-making pottery among its facilities (Plate 21).

In the early Imperial era, the estate production
of amphorae would have been mixed in with that of
domestic pottery vessels, bricks, and tiles. Most of
these latter items would have been used on the estate
itself, though surpluses may have found their way to
the local marketplace. As for a workforce, slaves
there were aplenty at least through the early part of
the 1st century A.D. Thereafter, however, as the
expense of buying and maintaining slaves began to
rise, landowners found ample numbers of recently
freed men who were desperately in need of work to
feed and clothe their families. Fully fledged citizens
though these men were, estate owners did not hesitate to lay them off if they fell ill or if a lengthy
spell of bad weather disrupted the farm's daily routine or crop yield.

Things seem to have changed by the early
Byzantine era. The pool of slaves had shrunk
appreciably over the intervening years, and the daily
lot of much of the Roman citizenry was moving
towards serfdom, amid an increasingly oppressive
amount of State bureaucracy and local taxation.
One mid 3rd century A.D. papyrus from the
Egyptian town of Oxyrhynchus—then the capital
of the Aegyptus province—describes how a potter
leased an estate's workshop so that he could provide
the estate's owner with some 18,000 wine amphorae
over a two year period (Plate 22). Leases of this
kind were, in effect, labor contracts and have

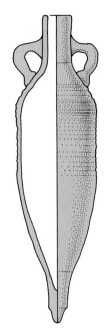

PLATE 23:

Although surely manufactured along the Nile in Egypt and popular in Alexandria, examples also were common at sites in northern Africa. The type designation is named for Egloff, the excavator of Kellia (near modern Benghazi) in Libya (Egloff 1977). Its form persisted from the late 4th to the mid 6th century A.D. (Peacock and Williams 1986). Its capacity of about 1.28 U.S. gallons [4.9 liters] is close to current estimates of the value of the *chous* (see Plate 22).

Egloff 177 amphora

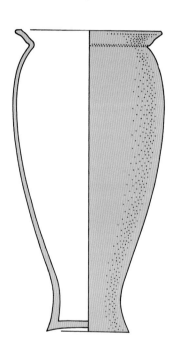

PLATE 24:

This thin-walled pottery beaker (Ht., 5.5 inches) dates to the third-quarter of the 1st century B.C. and comes from Cosa (near modern Orbetello). Its production was all but eclipsed in the Augustan era when glassworkers imitated its form, the novelty of glass's transparency carrying the day for the latter industry (Moevs 1973: see also Endnote 26).

parallels with various rental agreements of the day, including those which allowed for growing crops in the vineyard itself in exchange for some cash and some in-kind payment of wine and other provisions.

Again, one cannot help but be struck by the scale of production; the amphorae produced by way of this lease alone would have held about 81,000 U.S. gallons of wine. If the land area committed to wine production in Roman Aegyptus was roughly what it has been in recent years in modern Egypt—about 19,800 acres—and if the yield was close to what was typical for ancient Italy—about 220 U.S.

gallons per acre [1 *culleus* per *iugerum*: see VI: The Virtuous Vine]—estate-owned potteries along the Nile would have been making close to 900,000 amphorae every year.

Only a fraction of the wine would have been consumed on the estates themselves. Some of it would have gone to satisfy the domestic demands of nearby towns; some of it would have been sent quite profitably to the numerous military forts scattered along the length of the Nile. Some also would have traveled far further afield, supplying the citizenry of Alexandria or being shipped out of there to various ports around the Mediterranean basin (Plate 23).

Clearly then the manufacture of amphorae was a major Roman industry, and one of a scale that always would be swayed by the year-to-year state of wine production throughout the Roman World. That will have been true also wherever wooden casks (*cupa*) rather than pottery amphorae were the preferred means of storage.[25] Other craft industries were affected by such matters as well. Someone had to make the various kinds of bottles that stored wine and wine-based sauces in the kitchen of every home; someone had to make all the beakers and jugs that were used throughout the day in each city tavern and those that were brought out during every family's evening meal. Someone had to keep quartermasters of frontier armies supplied with such vessels as well. When the population of the Empire approached 54 million during the reign of the emperor Trajan around A.D. 116, potters and glassblowers combined probably were producing as many as 100 million wine-related vessels every year, just to keep pace with normal household wear-and-tear and tipsied carelessness (Plates 24-27).[26]

In those years when grape harvests caused poets to wax lyrical about the bounty of the vine, everyone drank well and some grew a little richer. If things went drastically wrong with the wine industry, however, it was not just the vintners that suffered. When in A.D. 197 a vengeful emperor Septimius Severus turned his back on Spain, many of the potteries and glassblowing workshops of the province of Baetica surely were ruined.[27] Whenever plague struck the Roman World—which it did several times over the centuries—it ravaged the populations of cities, forts, and farmlands alike.[28] Potteries and glassblowing workshops throughout the Empire were crippled for lack of a workforce and lack of healthy customers.

PLATE 25:

This kind of cylindrical glass vessel (Ht., 4.6 inches), with its simple wrap-around thread of decoration, seems to have been *the* most popular wine beaker in Rome's Eastern Mediterranean provinces during the second half of the 4th century A.D. We know it was produced in large quantities at the glassworking center of Jalame in Israel though it is likely that there were other production sites in Egypt as well (Weinberg 1988).

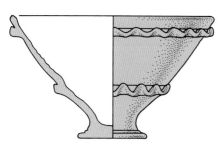

"Pie-crust" decorated cup
Trier, grave 132: 1st half of 2nd century A.D.

Bulbous-bodied beaker
Trier, grave 184: 1st half of 4th century A.D.

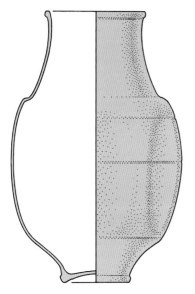

Indented bulbous beaker
Trier, grave 167: 2nd half of 3rd century A.D.

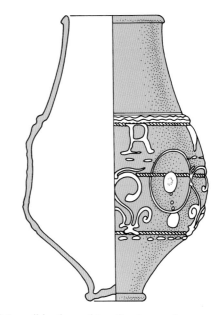

"Motto" beaker, white slip decoration
St. Albans: 1st half of 4th century A.D.

PLATE 26:

Some typical pottery wine vessels used in Rome's north-western provinces (after Goethert-Polaschek [1977] and Greene [1978])

The emperor Augustus's stimulation of the pottery-making industry during the last decade of the 1st century B.C. was extremely effective. The kilns of Arretium (modern Arrezzo) were much expanded, and the importation of enslaved, highly skilled potters from Asia Minor greatly improved ware quality. Within just a few decades, however, the pottery workshops of southern Gaul became dominant, and in subsequent decades the needs of the army led to the growth of major pottery-making centers close to the Rhine frontier (Greene 1986).

Wine flask
Trier, grave 75: late 1st century A.D.

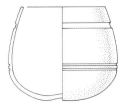

Globular cup: lathe-cut, grooved decoration
Hofheim type: late 1st century A.D.

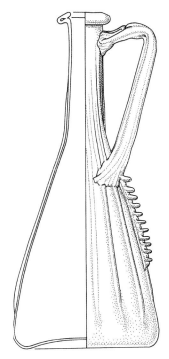

Conical jug: applied trails, ribbed decoration
Radnage, cremation burial: late 1st century A.D.

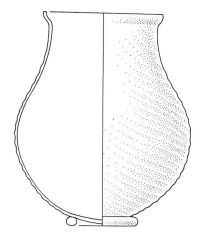

Bulbous, optic-blown beaker
Trier, grave 185: 1st half of 4th century A.D.

PLATE 27:

Some typical glass wine vessels used in Rome's northwestern provinces (after Goethert-Polaschek [1977] and
Harden [1987])
The Romans largely ignored glass until the end of the 1st
century B.C. Thereafter, however, the emperor Augustus'
policy of centralizing essential domestic crafts in the
Italian peninsula changed all that. Within decades Rome
and towns around the Bay of Naples had thriving glassworking industries in their outskirts. Importation of
enslaved, highly skilled workers from the eastern
Mediterranaean provinces ensured a steady improvement of
ware quality (Fleming 1999). Like pottery-making, glassworking also eventually spread deeply into the northwestern provinces, Augusta Treverorum and Colonia Agrippina
(modern Trier and Cologne, respectively) emerging as primary production centers by the 2nd century A.D.

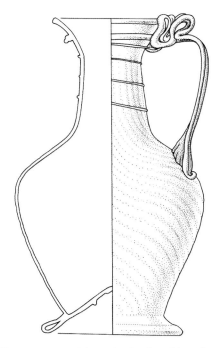

Wine jug: optic-blown body, fluted handle
Cologne, N5947: 1st half of 4th century A.D.

Cardamom (*Elettaria cardomomum*)

Tucca, what satisfaction do you get out of mixing must stored in Vatican jars with old Falernian? What great good have vile wines done you or fine wines what harm? Never mind about us; it's a crime to murder Falernian and put fierce toxins into a Campanian vintage. Maybe your guests deserved to perish, but so costly a jar did not deserve to die.

(Martial, *Epigrams* I.18)

IX

CHANGING THE FLAVORS

THE ROMANS WERE PROUD OF THEIR KNOWLEDGE OF VITICULTURE. A forward-thinking Roman landowner would encourage his *vinitor* to experiment with different methods of vine grafting and training, all in search of that special vintage, and that special flavor which would separate one producer from the next. The vines that yielded the quality wines, such as Falernian and Caecuban, were encouraged to clamber their way up tall Campanian poplars and elms. (The farmhands who picked those grapes had to do the same, risking life and limb for the most precious bunches.) Other vines were cultivated according to some worthy aspect of their growth, among them "The *visula*, better suited to very low frames, make very little wood but tough broad leaves, whose size affords the fruit very good protection against hail. . . ." (Columella, *On Agriculture* III.ii)

Agricultural scholars carefully described what they knew about the kinds of grape that grew best in certain regions of the Empire, categorizing them by shape and manner of clustering, and by their potential flavor both for wine-making and as a fresh fruit.

> The Dyrrachini [of southern Dalmatia] speak highly of the *balisca* vine, which the Spanish provinces call *coccolobis*; its grapes grow in rather scanty bunches and can stand hot weather and southern winds; its wine is apt to go to the head, but the yield is abundant. (Pliny, *Natural History* XIV.30)

You will recall that this "cox-comb" grape eventually was to find its way into Gaul and become the foundation of the modern viticulture of Bordeaux (see XVII: Epilogue).

PLATE 28:

Rehovot in the red soil hills of Judaea (see Plate 12) provides us with one of the best-preserved wine-presses of the early Byzantine era, albeit an elaborate one for its day. It is certainly a more complicated structure than was used in Republican and early Imperial times (Ahlström 1978; Rossiter 1981). The various components of this press yielded several kinds of wines as each grape harvest was brought to it (Roll and Ayalon 1981):
- Baskets of grapes were piled up in plaster-lined compartments (*tabulata*) – six of them in this instance. The juice which exuded from the grapes under the pressure of their own weight was used to make a sweet, heavy wine of the highest quality (*protropum*).
- The grapes were transferred to the treading floor (*forum vinarium*), and crushed by bare-footed work men who walked back and forth, sometimes leaning on one another, sometimes keeping their balance by holding onto an overhead beam. The fresh juice (*mustum*) flowed off the floor through a stone channel that connected to an intermediate vat. A jar was recessed into this vat's floor to collect dregs carried along by the wine's flow. The *mustum* then poured through a clay pipe that led into one of two deeper settling vats (*lacus musti*). In each *lacus*, there was a two-part sedimentation system comprising a large basin hewn into the bedrock with a deeper hole at its center that contained another dreg-collecting jar. The owner of each batch of *mustum*—we assume that as large a press as this one served more than one vineyard—would have been responsible for decanting it into the large jars (*dolia*) in which the primary fermentation would take place.
- The once-pressed grapes were stacked on a cylindrical limestone slab (*arca lapidum*) recessed into the center of the treading floor. This slab formed the lower part of a mechanical press. The upper part probably was a wooden slab with four handles pinned into it. Each slab was mounted on a thick vertical screw (see INSET). The juice gathered from this press was called *mustum tortivum*. It was considered of inferior quality. When flavored with rosemary and stored for a couple of months, however, it could become a passable medicinal tonic (see Columella, *On Agriculture* XII.xxxvii).

One might imagine that there was little else of value in twice-crushed grapes, but it was common practice for them to be mixed with water to yield a mediocre wine (*lora*) that was included in the daily rations of an estate's laborers. The grape skins and other waste (*vinaceum*) from the press also were used as cattle fodder or fertilizer (see Cato, *On Agriculture* XXV amd LIV).

Rehovot's "twin-slab and screw" kind of press was quite unsophisticated for its day (Dayagi-Mendels 1999). Even by the mid 1st century A.D., much larger presses that worked on a "lever-and-drum" principle were fully developed in Italy (see Drachmann [1932], interpreting Pliny, *Natural History* XVIII.317), as were ones that worked on a "lever-and-screw" principle (see Plate 76).

INSET

"Grape treading and pressing": detail from a 6th century A.D. mosaic floor at Mt. Nebo in Israel

PLATE 29:

THE FINAL WINE EXTRACT—*lora*

To make wine for the farm-hands to drink through winter, pour into a jar 10 *quadrantalia* of must, add 2 *quadrantalia* of sharp vinegar, 2 *quadrantalia* of *sapa*, and 50 *quadrantalia* of fresh water. Stir with a stick three times a day for five consecutive days. Then add 64 *sextarii* of old sea water, cover the jar, and seal it ten days later. This wine will last until the summer soltice; whatever is left over after the soltice, it will be a very sharp and excellent vinegar. (Cato, *On Agriculture* CIV)
[1 quadrans = 2.9 U.S. ounces or 82 grams] [1 sextarius = 1.14 U.S. pints or 0.54 liters]
• *sapa* was must that had been boiled down to about a third of its original volume (Solomon 1995)
So this recipe produced about 44 U.S. pints of *lora*. This drink is similar to the reputedly invigorating *posca* which was provided Roman troops when normal wine rations were in short supply (Giacosa 1992).

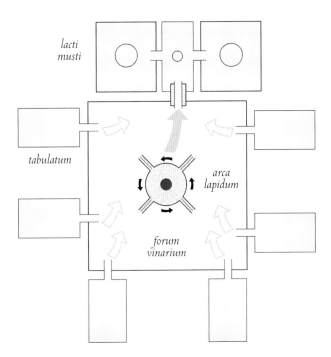

The "twin-sisters" vine (*gemellarum*) of Aminae, from the Apulia region at Italy's "heel" that yielded wine which was top-ranked for its body and aging qualities, and one of the most heavily exported from Italy (see Plate 9); the *eugenia* vine from the Taormina hills of Greece that transplanted so successfully to Alba; the thorn vine (*spionia*) that thrived in the foggy hillsides around Ravenna—all these special vines, and dozens of others provided the general citizenry's *vin ordinaire*.[29] They were documented so well that we have a real sense of the sophistication of the Roman wine palate and the care taken by Roman vintners to cater to it.[30]

The successful vintner would waste very little of any year's harvest, savoring the first extract of extremely sweet wine and gathering even the final squeezings as a vintage of sorts that might nourish his slaves (Plates 28 and 29). Again to avoid any waste, portions of better wine batches sometimes would be blended with mediocre ones. More likely, though, the failings of an inferior wine would be masked deliberately by the addition of some herb or other—whatever might appeal to the inquisitive tastes of the popular market. Many of these herbs were simply the ones to be found on the local hillsides, such as gentian, valerian, and hazelwort; or the ones that could be carefully tended in a small kitchen garden, such as rue, marjoram, and even the bitterly flavored thyme. Certain shrubs, such as juniper, germander, and myrtle, were popular for this purpose as

Myrtle (*Myrtus communis*)

PLATE 30:

To make a syrup from this evergreen shrub, the Greeks would "boil tender sprigs of myrtle, with the leaves still on them, in a salted must, and after pounding them, boil down one *librum* of the mixture in three *congii* of must, until only two *congii* remain. The drink made by the same process from the berries of the wild myrtle is called myrtle wine; this stains the hands." (Pliny, *Natural History* XIV.104)
[1 *librum* = 0.71 U.S. pounds 1 *congius* = 6.84 U.S. pints]
Because of it sweet scent, myrtle also was used as a cosmetics ingredient and in some medical prescriptions, including one to suppress bad breath (see Pliny, *Natural History* XXV.175) and another that involved a near-ritualistic preparation of a myrtle wine that could be used to treat colic and looseness of the bowels (see Columella, *On Agriculture* XII.xxxviii).

well (Plate 30). Wealthy folk made a point of buying wines that had been spiced with herbs that were imported from afar—saffron from Cilicia in Asia Minor, cardamom from the Malabar Coast of India, and resinous myrrh from Arabia, so that a supper table must at times have smelled more like a perfume store than a place to eat.[31]

Then there is the matter of using pitch as a flavoring. All amphorae and wooden casks used to transport wine were pitch-lined and -sealed within, so presumably any vintage would take up at least a hint of a resinous flavor during a lengthy storage period.[32] But that was a far cry from deliberately blending pitch into the wine at the outset of its fermentation. As we find today in people's reactions to Greek *retsina*, resinated wines appealed to some Romans—they liked the piquant flavor and enjoyed the pleasant scent it added to the wine's general bouquet. Others, however, loathed it—"The little wine they have in their country [Gaul] is mixed with pitch, and harsh." (Strabo, *Geography* IV.6)—no wasted sentiment there.

We know that the Romans imported a great deal of pitch-flavored wine from the region of Vienne on the Rhône—perhaps some of its critics were showing the usual Roman anti-Gallic prejudice when they so readily dismissed it (see Plate 16)—but it also was produced in significant quantities in the region of Bruttium (in essence, the "toe" of the Italian peninsula), and surely was drunk there with pleasure.[29] Most everyone agreed, however, that

resinated wine was good for you, at minimum working against an acidic wine's tendency to cause a sickening headache (*crapula*). Doctors thought that it helped to cure stomach ailments that they described as a paralysis (*resolutio*) that led to rejection of food ". . .so that the nutrition of the body is wont to cease, and so it is consumed by wasting." (Celsus, *On Medicine* IV.12)

Admittedly, amid all the practical experience and scholarship about how to achieve the best results in wine-making, there was a lot of folklore floating around as well. Vintners would encourage the growths of certain herbs, such as black hellebore and hyssop, to entwine themselves amongst the vine's branches; the idea was that the herb would transfer its flavor to the grape in some way, by sheer proximity. It was thought that certain astrological elements could effect the wine production process as well.

> . . . must of new wine should be boiled when there is no moon, which means at the conjunction of that planet, and not on any other day. (Pliny, *Natural History* XIV.136)[33]

The inclusion of these notions in the otherwise quite conservative literature on Roman viticulture should not jar our modern sensibilities too much. We surely can understand that any Roman who had waited so patiently for his vineyard to mature and become profitable was never going to risk the loss of a vintage simply for lack of attention to a tradition-steeped ritual, however idiosychratic its basis.

There, when the wine is set, you will tell me many a tale—how your ship was all but engulfed in the midst of the waters; and how, while hastening home to me, you feared neither hours of unfriendly night nor headlong winds of the south. . . .

(Ovid, *The Amores* II.xi)

"Banquet of Dido and Aeneas": vignette from the
Vergilius Romanus ms.
6th century A.D.

X

WINE TO EASE THE TONGUE

UP TO THIS POINT I HAVE FOCUSED ONLY ON MATTERS RELATED TO WINE'S PRODUCTION. Since it was undertaken in large measure in response to popular, sometimes fleeting tastes, the flavoring of wine is a comfortable bridge to the other end of my story— wine's consumption and the pleasure taken in it. As it happens, herbalism will come up again in discussion of the Roman use of wine for medicinal purposes. For now, however, let us stay with the idea of wine's pleasures.

Century after century, Rome's great poets and philosophers extolled the virtues of relaxing with friends to enjoy good conversation and good wine. The more romantic writers—notably, the late Republican poet, Horace—wrote of the finest of wines being savored in idyllic settings, such as by a quiet river bank or under the shade of beautifully flowering trees.[34] For most Romans, though, the family dinner table would have been the usual place for such relaxation. Everyone in the house had been up since dawn, and those who had gone into fields or had business in the city's marketplace sustained themselves through the day with little more than a light lunch of bread and fruit, and a beaker of well-diluted *vin ordinaire*.

The slow rhythm of a late afternoon meal at home, however, was an opportunity to enjoy a slightly better quality wine, surely savored by those who could afford it. Most likely everywhere, in the city or the countryside, the conversation was of our own "kitchen table" variety. Among the poor, for whom most meals

PLATE 31:

RECIPES FOR *mulsum*

You will put 10 *libra* of best honey into an *urna* of must and after mixing them carefully together, you will store the must in a flagon and immediately seal it up with plaster and order it to be placed in a loft [to ferment for a month]. (Columella, *On Agriculture* XII.xli)

[1 *libra* = 0.72 U.S. pounds   1 *urna* (half an *amphora*) = 3.42 U.S. gallons]

Columella also recommended that the must be *protropum*, i.e., the juice gathered before the grapes were trodden (see Plate 28). Pliny (*Natural History* XXII.113) suggested, however, that the fresh must be replaced by an already fermented, older wine. This would have given the mulsum a somewhat drier flavor.

consisted of a ground wheat gruel known as *puls*, talk would turn to their plight, and to current stories of the Mediterranean piracy which might deny them their State-provided grain dole. In a craftsman's home, everyday concerns would be about health, uncertainty of employment, and the truancy of the children. How much wine was on the table there would give a good indication of how much work was available to the householder at the time. In a businessman's home, there would be grumblings about the iniquities of the latest gimmick in State taxation and an occasional celebration for a venture well-completed. (Such a venture might well have included the shipment of wines from afar; in which case, some judicious tastings would have been in order.) Whatever the social setting, wine would loosen the tongue in familiar enough ways, some folk becoming garrulous and light-hearted, others intense and aggressively dogmatic.

If the Romans had any conventions similar to those of our Western world today—red wine with beef, white with poultry and fish, etc.—I don't know of them. But there was a reasonably well-established etiquette for wine's consumption during a Roman dinner of substance. A guest might expect first to be served some hors d'oeuvres, then a honeyed wine (*mulsum*)—in essence, a mead (Plate 31). Its intense sweetness would offset the saltiness of the fish and pig's feet that, along with hard-boiled eggs and stuffed artichokes, often were included among the appetizers.[35]

Somewhat better wines would be offered after each of the subsequent two courses—*mensa prima*, which would be meat-, poultry- or fish-based; and *mensa secunda*, which would be fresh fruit, a custard,

or some honey-sweet dessert (Plate 32). The last wine might be shared as dusk approached; the realization that another day was drawing to a close would mellow the party's mood.

Of course, there were those folk who had no family hearth to go to; and there were those who simply preferred not to go to it. Like most everyone else, these folk spent their mid-afternoon at the public baths (*thermae*)—exercising, gossiping, and enjoying a rejuvenating massage. The public baths of most towns were sizable places; the bathing areas were surrounded by several arcades that would be filled throughout the day with the bustle and noise of vendors trying to drum up casual trade for pastries and bowls of fresh greens. As the bulk of the now well-scrubbed citizenry wended their way home, however, the atmosphere of these arcades would change; their bars and restaurants were brought to life at dusk by the chatter and laughter of the remainder of the thermae's clientele.

Though there are only a few comments in Roman literature to substantiate my view, I believe that much of the fare offered in the eating houses of the thermae was "finger food" in the modern Western sense of the phrase—much of it greasy and spicy, such as the well-peppered sausages known as *Lacunicae* (Plate 33) and rissoles which comprised some ground meat and wine-soaked bread wrapped in a layer of pork fat (*omentum*). We might anticipate that the rissole meat was of somewhat dubious quality and condition; yet the gourmet Apicius, whose recipes I frequently cite here, first recommends peacock be used for this delicacy, then in order of lesser preference, pheasant, rabbit, chicken, or suckling pig (see his *De Re Coquinaria*, Book II on minced meats). As for

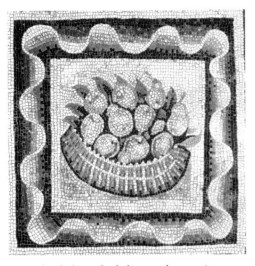

Detail of the *Sala degli animali* mosaic.

PLATE 32:

PEAR PATINA
From Apicius' *De Re Coquinaria*: recipe 162
> *Ingredients*: four pears, white wine, pinches of cumin and pepper, 1 Tbs. of honey, half a cup of *passum*, 3 eggs, and 1 Tbs. of olive oil.
> *Preparation*: Poach the whole pears in white wine, peel and core them, then crush them into a puree, mixing in the honey, spices and *passum*. Beat the eggs, then blend them into the pear puree with the olive oil. Bake in a casserole for about 20 minutes (after Giacosa 1992).

MAKING RAISIN WINE (*passum*)
 . . .clear away the rotten berries and put them aside; and afterwards hang the sound grapes on poles. Arrange that the poles shall always be in the sun, and when the berries are sufficiently withered, pull them off and tread them well. When you have made one layer of them, sprinkle old wine upon it, and then tread another layer of them on top and also sprinkle wine on it. In like manner tread a third layer and after pouring wine upon it, let it float on the top for five days; afterwards tread with your feet and squeeze the grapes in a new wicker basket. (Columella, *On Agriculture* XII.xxxix)
Though Columella does not say as much, presumably the juices that oozed from the basket were then sealed in an amphora to ferment for a month or so. This wine would have been extraordinarily sweet and potent.

PLATE 33:

SMOKED SAUSAGE (*Lucanica*)
From Apicius' *De Re Coquinaria*: recipe 61 (see Giacosa 1992)
 Ingredients: Ground pepper, cumin, summer savory, rue, parsley, bay berries, and fish sauce [*garum*]; minced belly pork, peppercorns, plenty of fat [*abundanti pinguedine*], pine nuts, and a stretched-thin length of intestine.
 Preparation: Grind the herbs and spices together with some of the fish sauce, then mix in the meat until everything is thoroughly blended. Add the rest of the fish sauce, the peppercorns, fat, and pine nuts, then squeeze the mixture into the sausage casing, and smoke it over an open fire.
Though now regarded as a northern Italian delicacy, the popularity of this sausage, along with its name, originated with Roman soldiers who had been served it in Lucania at the "heel" of Italy (Dalby & Grainger 1996). It usually was eaten with some bland side-dish such as wheat polenta (see Martial, *Epigrams* XIII.35).

their greasiness, if some of the obscene parts of Petronius' *Satyricon* are to be given credence, the residuals of the *omentum* often finished up being rubbed off on the hair of an attendant slave boy.

Which wines were drunk with such foodstuffs is not known; their fattiness would just about destroy anyone's palate for any reasonable vintage. But tavern fare could be more healthy and delicate than Lacunicae and the like. The countryside surrounding every Roman city offered a fine range of cheeses, fresh and smoked, that could be mixed with water and cracked wheat and some herbs to make delicious cakes that would go well with a robust local wine. And there were sweet wine-flavored biscuits that were particularly popular in the informal setting of a thermae's tavern when served with shavings of herb-stuffed pork (Plate 34).[36]

Roman taste, at least during the Republican and Early Imperial eras, leaned heavily towards sweeter wines which, because they were made from later season grapes, tended to be quite alcoholic.[37] To drink such strong wines neat was to be deemed "barbarian." Many writers noted that

was exactly what the Scythians of the Balkans would do; as would the Germanic peoples of northwestern Europe when they weren't swilling rough beer. The Romans took their lead from long-standing Greek customs, adding at least some measure of water to the wine or, in elite circles, a few ladles of melting snow. The degree of dilution applied probably depended on the setting. While entertaining friends within the home, around quarter strength would be normal; among a raucous crowd in the city's tavern, maybe the etiquette of dilution was forgotten altogether.

Detail of the *Sala degli animali* mosaic.

PLATE 34:

STUFFED LEG OF BOAR

From Apicius' *De Re Coquinaria*: recipe 339, which was dedicated to a famous cook of the day, named Terentius (Giacosa 1992).

Ingredients: a boar's leg (which would weigh about 4 U.S. pounds), a couple of bay twigs, and a bunch of fresh dill.

For the stuffing: two handfuls of rue, some garlic cloves, five bay berries, some peppercorns, 2 Tbs. of *garum*, half a cup of *caroenum*, and half a cup of olive oil.

Preparation: Pass a round stick along the joint of the leg, to separate the skin from the meat, and so allow the seasoning to be poured into the space through a small funnel. Grind together the peppercorns, bay berries and rue; then add, to personal taste, some fine *garum*, *caroenum*, and drops of olive oil. Once the meat is stuffed, the filled part is fastened with flax string, and placed in a cauldron. It is boiled in sea water with bay twigs and dill.

MAKING MUST CAKES (*mustacei*)

Moisten one *modius* of wheat flour with wine must; add aniseed, cumin, two *libra* of lard, one *libra* of cheese, and the bark of a laurel twig. When you have made them into cakes, put bay leaves under them, and bake. (Cato, *On Agriculture* CXXI)

[*modius* = 18.2 U.S. pints (dry measure)   1 *libra* = 0.72 U.S. pounds]

You mix Veientan for me and serve Massic for yourself. I had rather smell these cups than drink.

(Martial, *Epigrams* III.49)

Small jugs for table service: Cold water will not be lacking, nor warm either, when you ask for it. But forbear to dally with a pernickety thirst.

(Martial, *Epigrams* XIV.105)

Wine juglet of colorless glass with single-coiled threads applied at the neck
Late 4th century A.D.

XI

A MATTER OF ETIQUETTE

ETIQUETTE MAY HAVE BEEN ON SHAKY GROUND IN A TYPICAL ROMAN WINE BAR. It was upheld firmly, however, in a quite different setting for dining—the *convivium*. In Roman literature, the luxury usually associated with this kind of setting brings to mind the Greek *symposium* from which it obviously did derive some of its structure (Plate 35). But their common threads are somewhat superficial. While the Greeks went out of their way to ensure social equality among their invitees, a Roman patron would without hesitation host a convivium for his inferior *amici* and *clientes*—those associates, long-standing or briefly met, who might be the means to business and political advantage. Unlike the symposium, which was in essence solely a drinking bout that followed a meal, the convivium was decidely a banquet in our Western sense with emphasis on the richly prepared and novel food, the partaking of which was a pleasure (thus, a conviviality) which would be accompanied by a generous flow of wines.

PLATE 35:

In this 6th century A.D. dining scene known as *The Pharaoh's Banquet*, we can imagine a Roman host and his guests reclining for hours during the late afternoon, enjoying some wine while various bands of musicians, actors, mimes, and jugglers kept them amused (Dunbabin 1996).

The Roman *convivium*

Two lengthy works of the 2nd century A.D., Plutarch of Chaeronea's *Table Talk* and Athenaeus of Naucratis' *Banquet of the Philosophers*, provide us with detailed insight into the way a convivium might proceed throughout the evening. The dinner "parasite" (*grassator*) who accepted invitations most readily but never offered similar hospitality himself, and the pretentions of literary performances at private symposia—these were just two of the trappings of elegant Greek dining. The Romans mocked and rejected them, claiming meanwhile that the gradual lapse of the *symposium* into a lax, sometimes disorderly affair was why the Greeks had forsaken chairs and slid onto couches more forgiving of their eventual drunken state. Instead, they pointed with somewhat smug delight to the democratric character of the public feasts given by their own politicians and emperors, turning a blind eye to the fact that such events were as-often-as-not intended to influence voters.

The convivium was intended to be a joyous event.[38] Italian alkanet (*euphrosynum*, "the plant that cheers") was added to the wine, and vervain (*hiera botane*, "sacred plant") was sprinkled with water on the dining couches because it was believed that such measures somehow contributed to the gaiety of the guests (see Pliny, *Natural History* XXV.107). Invariably there would be music; at live-

lier gatherings there might be acrobats and mock gladiatorial battles. The aged Ummidia Quadratilla, even though it was socially frowned upon, maintained a troupe of pantomimes to perform at her own convivia as well as in the theater (Pliny the Younger, *Letters* VII.24).[39]

The convivium also was a place to be philosophical about matters of substance, even if, in the sober light of morning, such matters shrank somewhat in consequence. In this setting guests might get caught up in a discussion of the fables of Aesop as parables for real Roman life and of how best not to give offense to a freedman guest whose memories of enslavement were scarcely a few years past (*Table Talk* I.I and II.I, respectively). Amid all this chatter and banter would have been endless ponderings on the purpose and effects of wine in Roman society. This was a natural place to give credence to old wives' tales about wine's effect upon people's health.

And if the nature and power of wine were calorific, administering wine to sufferers of cardiac disorder would be, I think, like putting fire on snow. . . wine-lovers very soon in fact become old men, and many get bald at an early age and their hair turns grey before their prime. . . . (Plutarch, *Table Talk* III.5)

During a convivium it was the host's responsibility to sense when the interest in a particular topic was waning, and have some fresh question ready to keep the conversation bouyant—odd ones, sometimes, such as the perennially vexing which came first, the chicken or the egg (see Plutarch, *Table Talk* II.3). Was it right to strain wine?—some thought so, some thought not.[40] The issue of the appropriate dilution of wine also was debated intensely, often with brilliant scholarly recourse to literature, past and near-forgotten. Athenaeus (*Banquet of the Philosophers* X.426) makes it clear that Greek custom was to mix three parts of water with one of wine— thus, in social shorthand, a "Triton"—and it looks likely that Roman wine connoisseurs generally went along with that ratio. But one of Plutarch's guests, Aristion, argued humorously in favor of a three-to-two mix, claiming that it would be in perfect har-mony with the fifth concord of a lyre, to the tune of which so much drunken Bacchic revelry took place (see *Table Talk* III.9).

Three-to-one, three-to-two, whatever the mix, as far as I can tell, the convivium was, for the most part, an event for the wealthy. Throughout the Mediterranean World for much of the 1st millennium B.C., the furnishing of the banquet table with a range of beakers, jugs, ladles, and so on, inspired some of the finest of precious metal craftmanship, and the subsequent era of Roman dominance of that area kept those traditions fully intact (Plate 36).[41] No doubt there were socially aspiring merchants and minor State officials who contrived similarly structured dinner parties; to them we may attribute ownership of some equally well-crafted wine paraphernalia in bronze.

PLATE 36:

Silver cup (D., 4.9 inches, at rim) that was part of a full dining service found by chance in 1868 near Hildeshiem, in Germany

This service is thought to have belonged to a Roman commander who was campaigning against Germanic tribes on the Rhine frontier during the early 1st century A.D. (Oliver 1977). Despite the elegance of its decoration, with the tautly stretched ribbons and the loosely hanging garlands emphasizing so well the various curves of the vessel, this kind of cup attracted the scorn of one Roman poet who viewed it as yet another intrusion of foreign fancifulness into Roman traditional taste.

> Persian elegance, I hate, young man, and take no pleasure in garlands woven on linden bast. . .Strive not to add anything else to the plain myrtle! The myrtle befits us both—you, the servant, and me, the master, as I drink beneath the thick-leaved vine. (Horace, *Odes* I.xxxviii)

Whatever the material, however, there were two specific vessels that speak most strongly of differences in Greek and Roman attitudes towards the social role of wine. Among the numerous depictions of the symposium that occur on Greek Red Figure pottery vases during the 6th to 4th centuries B.C., the focus of the entire process of wine service is the *krater*. It was in such a massive vessel that the wine and the water was mixed at some distance from the banquetters. That way, everyone at a Greek symposium drank exactly the same wine—not just the same vintage, but in the same diluted state.

The krater appears at the Roman convivium as well, often with a form and decoration that clearly echoes its Greek inspiration (Plate 37). Next to it, however, there invariably would be a quite different vessel, the *authepsa*, a device for boiling water that could be drawn off as required (Plate 38). The Romans' introduction of the authepsa into the process of wine service meant that each guest could be offered his wine and his water quite separately. Each then could mix them to taste in his own cup.

This "customized" approach to the serving of wine was by no means adopted universally. One offhand comment in Plutarch's *Table Talk* (I.i)—"Indeed, just as the wine must be common to all, so too the conversation. . . ."—indicates clearly enough that some wealthy Romans during the early 2nd century A.D. still were clinging to, perhaps even trying to revive the Greek tradition. Just how much the use of an authepsa contributed to the versatility of a luxurious Roman convivium is clear, however, from the description of a special device that the politician-cum-philosopher, Marcus Terentius Varro, built in the aviary of his idyllic villa at Casinum (modern Cassino):

> On the island is a small column, and on the inside of it is a post which holds up, instead of a table, a wheel with spokes. . .This is revolved by a single servant in a way that everything to drink and eat is placed on it at once and moved around to all the guests. . .from this pond a stream runs into the two fish-basins. . .and minnows dart back and forth, while it is so arranged that cold and warm water flows for each guest from the wooden wheel. . . . (Varro, *On Agriculture* III.v)

Clearly to share wine with Varro was to be pampered in the extreme. Over the years, though, this kind of considerate behavior aroused some cynicism among certain banqueteers as to what motives lay behind such elaborate arrangements. Usually, it was just a complaint about the quality of wine being offered.

> And let the wine be the same for all guests—where is it laid down that he [the banquet's host] should get drunk on wine with a fine bouquet while I must burst my belly on new stuff? (Lucian, *Saturnalia*. 22)

At other times, however, the cynicism was colored by a healthy dose of fear, particularly if one moved in the very highest levels of Roman society. Wine's rich flavors could mask the bitterness of a poison such as aconite that, along with certain species of mushrooms, appears to have re-directed so frequently the course of imperial history. In A.D. 17, at the instigation of the emperor Tiberius, the governor of Syria, Calpurnius Piso, denied the latter's nephew, Germanicus, his place in the line of imperial succession by poisoning him. In A.D. 55, the emperor Nero removed his rival, Britannicus, in similar fashion, the latter's death throes being passed off rather unconvincingly as the result of an epileptic fit (see Suetonius, *Lives of the Caesars* IV.i and VI.xxxiii, respectively).

It would have called for ultra-confidence in one's favored status with the likes of the emperor Gaius (Plate 39) to attend one of his banquets, knowing that the wine beaker placed at your elbow just might be a hellebore-laced Falernian which could scarcely be refused without giving equally lethal imperial affront. True, in those frightening times, you could hire foretasters (*praegustatores*); they were sufficiently numerous to able to form a guild with their own officials. It has never been clear to me, however, why bringing your praegustator to an emperor's table was not interpreted as yet another kind of affront. Indeed, those praegustatores would have found themselves in an awkward, if not deadly

PLATE 37:

Silver *krater* (Ht., 14.2 inches) from the late 1st century B.C. Hildesheim Treasure
Wine-mixing vessels of this kind appear in many illustrations of Roman wine paraphernalia, among them a wall-painting in the tomb of Vestorius Priscus, at Pompeii,
where a krater stands at the center of an elegant display of silver drinking cups, jugs,
and ladles (Dunbabin 1993).
This *krater* has a capacity of about 31 *sextarii* [about 4.4 U.S. gallons]—not an
insignificant amount of wine even when diluted in proper Roman style. But those
depicted in later Roman scenes, such as the 3rd century A.D. *Opora, Agros and Oinos at
Dinner* mosaic from the "House of the Boat of Psyches" at Antioch, appear far larger,
sometimes standing waist-high to the guests (Kondoleon 2000).

PLATE 38:

This bronze *authepsa* (Ht., 14.6 inches) probably came from a doctor's depot in
the lower town of Augusta Raurica (modern Augst) in Switzerland. It dates to
the 1st century A.D. Literary sources indicate that these water-heating devices were
luxury items in the Roman world (Dunbabin 1993). For example, in 80 B.C., the
fast-rising young lawyer, Marcus Tullius Cicero, in his attack on the rich freedman
Chrysogonus noted that the latter had a house crammed with Delian and Corinthian
vessels ". . .among them that self-cooker (*authepsa*), which he recently bought at so high
a price that passers-by, hearing the auctioneer crying out the bids, thought that an
estate was being sold." (Cicero, *In Defense of Sextus Roscius of Ameria* XLVI.131)

PLATE 39:

Gold coin (*aureus*) depicting the emperor Gaius (reigned, A.D. 37–41)

Today this emperor (self-styled as Caligula) is perhaps best known for his bizarre plan to give consular rank to his favorite racehorse, Incitatus.

In A.D. 38, aided and abetted by a prefect of the watch, Macro, Caligula set out to murder his already sick brother, Gemellus. But he suspected that the latter had taken a precautionary antidote—actually it was a cough mixture—prompting the remark: "What? an antidote against Caesar?" So, to hastened matters along, he suffocated Gemellus with a pillow instead (see Suetonius, *Lives of the Caesars* IV.xxix).

PLATE 40:

Gold coin (*aureus*) depicting the emperor Nero (reigned, A.D. 54–68)

The prefect, Sextus Afranius Burrus, was the man who led Nero to the Praetorian Guard and so ensured his rise to power. Two historians record, however, that in A.D. 55 Burrus' eventual reward was to have his palate smeared with a poisonous paste that ostensibly was a remedial throat medicine (see Suetonius, *Lives of the Caesars* VI.xxxv; and Tacitus, *Annals* XIV.li.).

position, if a poison were carefully disguised as a fashionable medication sent to a rival's bedside by a falsely solicitous emperor (Plate 40).

Not even saints-to-be were immune from such risk. In the 6th century A.D., Pope Gregory recounted how a group of disgruntled monks conspired to poison their spiritual leader at dinner, only to be defeated by something akin to a miracle.

When the glass cup which contained the fatal drink was offered to the Father who was reclining at table, to be blessed according to monastic ceremony, Benedict [of Nursia] extended his hand to trace the sign of the Cross. The fatal cup, which he was holding at some distance, broke as if he had hurled a stone against it. . . . (St. Gregory, *Dialogues* II.3)

If the plotters had been successful, the Christian Church would have lost the man who came to be known as the Patriarch of Western monasticism. Such are the twists of fate in life.

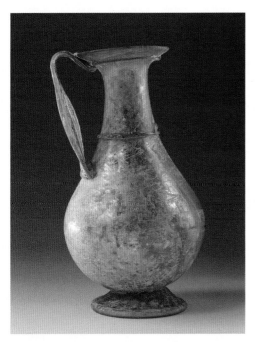

For song, laughter, and dancing are characteristic of men who drink wine in moderation; but babbling and talking about what is better left in silence is at once the work of actual intoxication. . . .

(Plutarch, *Table Talk* III.introduction)

Anyone who thinks that Acerra reeks of yesterday's wine misses his guess. Acerra always drinks till sunrise.

(Martial, *Epigrams* I.28)

Wine pitcher of green glass with a strap-handle; capacity of 2 *sextarii*
4th century A.D.

XII

DRUNKENNESS AND DEPRAVITY

LET US RETURN TO EVENTS OF THE EARLY IMPERIAL ERA. The *convivium*, with its emphasis on food (and, in reality, on simple entertainment and fluid conversation) was one thing; the *comissatio* was quite another. This was truly a drinking party that most likely took those guests who were still around at the end of a convivium far into the night hours and assuredly put them deep into their cups. I suspect that good manners often still prevailed, so the wine still was diluted in appropriate measure. But the sheer quantity of alcohol consumed would have taken its toll. We know nothing of the kind of conversations that occurred during a comissatio. Let's just guess that a raucous host encouraged a raucous chatter; a whining host, a whining chatter; and, sadly, that some fine wines were consumed at a time when no one's palate was really in any state to appreciate them.

Did the Romans drink a lot of wine? As the wine scholar, André Tchernia, noted some years ago, there is only one text—an inscription of A.D. 153 for the College of Aesculapius and Hygia on the Via Appia—that provides us any data on the wine consumption of Rome's citizenry, and then only for its adult male constituency. The senior members of that college were allocated a higher wine

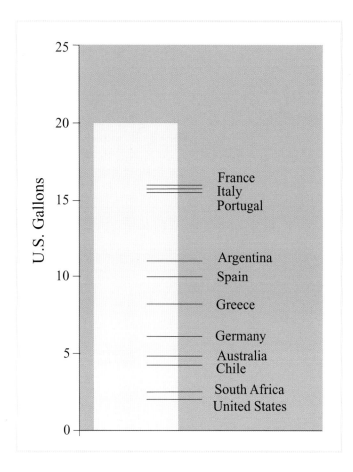

PLATE 41:

These data represent the per capita consumption that were recorded in 1996 for several major wine-producing countries (Robinson 1999). The 15.7 U.S. gallons per year cited for Italy is averaged over the entire population. Working backwards and making some reasonable assumptions—that pre-adolescents drink very little wine, and that adolescents and adult women usually drink only half as much wine as adult men—a figure emerges of about 24.7 U.S. gallons per year as the typical consumption of a modern Italian man.

It is true that, on average, such a man also drinks 11.0 U.S. gallons of beer per year (www.alcoweb.com), something almost all Romans would have regarded as barbaric. It is true too, that that Italians produce and drink quite a lot of home-grown wine that never appears in the official tax-based estimates. But this untaxed share of the market surely is nowhere near sufficient to add the 80 U.S. gallons per year required for a modern Italian man to match the consumption of his ancient counterpart.

ration than every one else—9 *sextarii* a day, which is equivalent to about 470 U.S. gallons per year. Rank-and-file members of the college were provided with much less—just 2 *sextarii* a day, which is equivalent to about 104 U.S. gallons per year. Italians are still among the leaders of wine consumption today, but adult males have a typical intake of only about 25 U.S. gallons per year, i.e., scarcely a quarter of that of their ancient predecessors (Plates 41 and 42). So, admittedly on the basis of the flimsiest of ancient data, the answer to the question is that, by modern standards, indeed they did.

Unhealthy though such a high consumption would have been, we should hesitate to censure such behavior too quickly. There seems little doubt that most Romans drank wine simply because the water being piped into their cities was none too pure and sometimes disease-ridden. And I would not be the first to suggest that general urban squalor—grim sanitary conditions, mold and mildew in shoddily built and poorly maintained apartments, etc.—

drove many a poor Roman to drown his sorrows. One poet observed "Who, after his wine, harps on the hardships of campaigns or poverty?" (Horace, *Odes* I.xviii), to which the most realistic answer would have been "almost anyone who experienced these conditions, until they were too drunk to remember them."

Did some Romans drink too much wine?—again, in modern health and moral terms, probably so. The social conflict inherent in consuming alcohol, moderate versus excess, was well recognized and the subject of dozens of literary comments ranging from high-minded metaphors that set good against evil to simple questions as to whether a hangover was worth the excesses that brought it about. Alcoholism could even be put forward as a legal defense, though somewhat cautiously, and as an excuse for criminal tendencies (Plate 43).[42]

The state of drunkenness was thought by some philosophers to be a time when one could peer most clearly into a man's heart and soul—thus: "Bronze

PLATE 41, INSET

The calculation made by Tchernia (1986) for ancient Rome's wine consumption needs some revision in light of the most recent estimates of the age-structure of populatations in the ancient Roman World. This structure is markedly different from the present one for Italy, or indeed for any country in the Western World (Plate 42A). High infant mortality meant most pre-adolescents scarcely had chance to appreciate their mother' milk, let alone wine, before some disease carried them off. Moral strictures on women's drinking of the kind discussed in this book (see XIV: A Separate Standard) also leads me to reckon that women drank far less that their men-folk; generously perhaps, about a fifth as much.

Thus, for Rome's citizenry of 700,000 people, the revised calculation would run as follows:

Population sector	Allowance	Wine consumed
Pre-adolescents (24.6%)	0 *sextarii* per day	zero
Adolescent females (10.1%)	0 *sextarii* per day	zero
Adolescent males (10.1%)	0.3 *sextarii* per day	21,210 *sextarii*
Adult females (27.6%)	0.3 *sextarii* per day	57,960 *sextarii*
Adult males (27.6%)	1.5 *sextarii* per day	289,800 *sextarii*

This yields a total consumption of 368,970 *sextarii* per day which is equivalent to about 19.2 million U.S. gallons per year (or 27.4 U.S gallons per capita).

The drinking habits of Rome's 300,000-strong slave population is hard to assess. Tchernia opted to cite the seasonally varied rations considered appropriate for slaves on Campanian farms (see Cato, *On Agriculture* LVII). But in such rural settings, slaves were regarded as chattels scarcely to be separated from the beasts of burden. In the cities, many slaves were integrated more closely into the household and usually better cared for; others were owned by the city itself, to work on construction projects, clean the public baths and temples, and sometimes do basic clerical work (Shelton 1988). All these slaves most likely received a fairly steady wine ration, while some may have frequented the taverns. The age structure of the Roman slave population is all but impossible to assess; the only certainty is that its life expectancy was lower even than that of the city's citizenry, maybe by as much as three or four years. If we assume minimal wine consumption for all young slaves and female slaves, and an adult male slave population of 75,000 each given I *sextarius* a day, their annual consumption would amount to 3.9 million U.S. gallons per year (or 1.3 U.S. gallons per capita).

Thus the average per capita wine consumption in ancient Rome was close to 23.1 U.S. gallons, which is considerably less than the Tchernia estimate of 48.2 U.S. gallons that is so often cited in the literature. Though my figure is only about 40% higher than the modern Italian per capita level of 15.7 U.S. gallons per year (see Plate 41), it should be born in mind that the social dynamics of each population are very different.

is the mirror of the outward form, wine the mirror of the mind." (Athenaeus, *Banquet of the Philosophers* x.427, attributed to Aeschylus). Meanwhile, a little too much wine, while recognized as a dangerous flame for lust or ill-timed impotence, was also accepted as a kind flame for romance and fondly-shared love.[43]

Playwrights and poets of old—among them Alcaeus of Lesbos who, in the 7th century B.C., was said to have offered good reasons for drinking heavily in every season; and Aeschylus of Athens, who was blamed for introducing the spectacle of drunken men into drama in the 5th century B.C.—were notorious for their drunkenness.[44] Some Romans credited that condition for the originality of the plays which were created, and some minor wordsmiths justified their drinking excesses through the example set by their literary heroes.[45] These play-

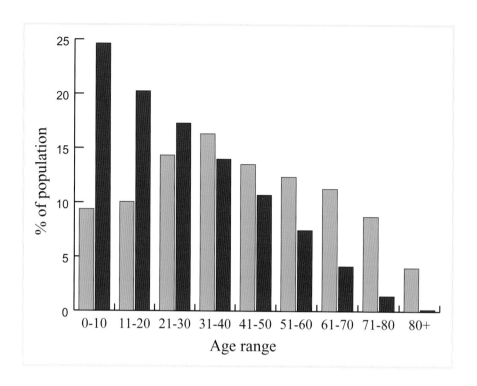

PLATE 42A:

A comparison of age distribution for the populations of Roman Egypt and modern Italy in 1999, based on data of Bagnell and Frier (1994), and the websites census.gov/ipc and photius.com. Expansion of the study of these modern data yields some interesting, though quite depressing facts:

Country	Population	Life expectancy, e(x)	Infant mortality rate
Italy	56.7 million	78.5 years	6.30 per 1000 births
Egypt	67.3 million	62.4 years	8.27 per 1000 births
Malawi	10.0 million	36.3 years	132 per 1000 births

Malawi ranks dead last (= 219th) for life expectancy in our world; we would have to go back to the end of the 19th century in Europe to find similar figures (biu.ac.il/~barilm/infant). For Roman Egypt [population, around 4.5 million], however, it has been estimated that there was an even higher infant mortality of close to 330 per 1000 births. Poor sanitation and overcrowded housing probably pushed that figure even higher in urban areas (Scobie 1986).

wrights themselves often used the device of the drunken servant who causes all sorts of problems for his master in comic routines that have echoes many centuries later; for example, in Shakespeare's portrayal of Sir Toby Belch's circle of friends in *Twelfth Night*. In this context, an observation such as "The one big trouble with wine is that it catches you by the feet first, it's a wrestler, a wily one. . . ." (Plautus, *Pseudolus* Act V.I), has a timeless quality to it.

Along with playwrights and their rival poets and scribblers, Roman satirists made the overindulgent senators, judges, and other government officials their main butt for jokes and criticism in broadsheets that were distributed throughout the city. To my knowledge, no one went so far as to do this to an emperor during his reign, though later writers were quick to heap on such criticisms once the grave stone sealed off a risk of immediate imperial retribution. Thus, the emperor Nero, whose modern

PLATE 42B:

The Romans understood well enough the possible brevity of their lives. A regular feature of Roman banquetry was a pause in the entertainment while the *larva convialis*—an articulated skeleton made of silver, ivory or wood—was laid before the guests. This reminded everyone that the joys of life were worldly and fleeting. The same idea underlies the depiction of skeletons as banqueteers on a silver goblet from the Boscoreale Treasure. The mood of the event is captured well by the following quotation:

> He threw it [the *larva*] down once or twice on the table, so that the supple sections showed several attitudes, and Trimalchio said appropriately: 'Alas for us poor mortals, that poor man is nothing. So we all shall be, after the world below takes us away. Let us live then, while it can go well with us.' (Petronius, *Satyricon*. 34)

notoriety hinges on his supposed responsibility for the burning of Rome in A.D. 64, was remembered in the period just after his suicide not so much for that event but rather for the extremes of his drink-enflamed debauchery and viciousness. If one Roman historian is to be believed:

> No sooner was twilight over than he [Nero] would catch up a cap or a wig and go to the taverns, or range about the streets playing pranks; which, however, were far from harmless. For he used to beat men as they came home from dinner, stabbing any of them who resisted him, and throwing them in the sewers. (Suetonius, *Lives of the Caesars* VI.xxvi)

Then there was the emperor Egalabalus, a Syrian who was only 14 years old when he came to power in A.D. 218 (Plate 44). He is reputed, among other things, to have once filled an entire pool with perfumed wine for he and his courtiers to bathe in, and to have had the canal around the circus filled with wine so that a naval spectacle could be mounted in it. This and innumerable other eccentricities—serving his courtiers with dinners made of glass, and eating the tongues of peacocks to stave

off the plague—made Egalabalus easy prey for the anonymous late 4th century editors of the encyclopaedic *The Augustan Histories*. There he is presented as having the vices of the earlier emperors, Tiberius, Caligula, and Nero, all rolled into one. In fact, in those chronicler's eyes, drunkenness emerges as one of the lesser failings of this emperor's blatantly immoral lifestyle.

Wealthy Romans drank what, for their palate, was the finest of wines—perhaps a wine made delicately aromatic by fine imported herbs (Plate 45), possibly even a champagne.[46] So there was always a temptation and a tendency to overdo consumption. A few of them, however, did recognize their weaknesses and took various steps to try and offset, or at least slow down, the onset of drunkenness. No doubt, somewhere among the courses served at a convivium, we would find foodstuffs equivalent to our mashed potatoes or milk, both of which now are recognized for the ability to slow the transfer of alcohol into the blood stream. But the Romans had other, less physiological tactics as well. Prime among them was the wearing of a crown of ivy, the plant symbolic of Bacchus and one said to have a "coldness" of nature that would check the fires of

PLATE 43:

In this Pompeian wall fresco, the artist depicts the hosts as quite unsurprised that one of their guests has to be carried out of the room in a drunken stupor, though as many Roman writers pointed out, such a state was socially unacceptable.

> You promise everything when you have drunk all night. In the morning you perform nothing. Drink in the morning, Pollio. (Martial, *Epigrams* XII.12)

SOME CLASSICAL QUOTATIONS ON DRUNKENNESS

We have two fountains beside us, one of which, the fountain of pleasure, one might liken to honey; the other, the sobering and wineless fountain of wisdom, to a well of homely and healthful water; these we must mix in the best possible way. (Athenaeus, *Banquet of the Philosophers* x.423)

Further, we have to seek not merely motives affecting the will, but also causes leading to error, such as drunkenness or ignorance. For just as such considerations lessen the guilt of a crime when regarded from the point of view of its quality, so they tell heavily against the criminal as far as the question of fact is concerned. (Quintilian, *Training in Oratory* VII.40)

From the western bounds of the world had come their foe Indulgence. . .as it chanced dawn was coming in and she was still reclining by the table when she heard the hoarse trumpets, and she stepped through the lukewarm cups, her foot slipping as she stepped through pools of wine and perfumes, and trampling on the flowers, and was making her drunken way to the war. (Prudentius, *The Poems*: Fight for Man's Soul)

It is not without occasion that physicians of experience do affirm that such as fill their gorges abundantly with meat and drink shall dream of dire and horrible sights. . . . (Lucius Apuleius, *The Golden Ass* I.18)

It is not so true that one of his [Aeschylus'] plays—the *Seven against Thebes*—is 'full of Ares,' to quote Gorgias, as that all of them are full of Dionysus. (Plutarch, *Table Talk* VII.10)

Wine ruins beauty, wine spoils youth, wine often causes a mistress to mistake her man. (Propertius, *Elegies* II.xxxiii)

PLATE 44:

A gold coin (*aureus*) depicting the emperor Elagabalus (reigned, A.D. 218–222)

It is some measure of the chaotic state of the Roman World during the first half of the 3rd century A.D. that it would be ruled by a 14 year old Syrian who was the hereditary priest of the Oriental sun god, Elagabal. In the space of just a four year reign, the bisexual antics and bizarre cult rituals of this youthful emperor shocked Roman sensibilities more intensely that any of the political savagery of many previous emperors (Scarre 1995).

PLATE 45:

Though this is an extremely bitter herb, it has been an ingredient of aperitifs and herbal wines for centuries past, including the Roman era: this, despite the fact that one of its principles, thujone, is toxic to the brain and the liver. Habitual use causes hallucinations and the kind of excitability made famous by the French artist, Vincent van Gogh, who surely was addicted to absinthe during the last years of his life.

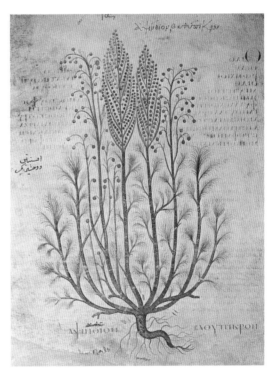

Pontic wormwood (*Artemisia absinthium*) from Dioscorides *De Materia Medica*

MAKING ROMAN ABSINTHE (*absintium*)

Use an *uncium* of clean ground wormwood from Pontus, one date from Thebes, 3 *scripulos* of mastic and of aromatic leaf, 6 *scripulos* of costus root, 3 *scripulos* of saffron, 18 *sextarii* of appropriate wine. It is necessary to use charcoal to remove its bitterness.
(Apicius' *De Re Coquinaria*: recipe 3: from Giacosa [1992])

[I *uncium* [a Roman ounce] = 0.95 U.S oz.   I *scripulos* [a scruple] = 0039 U.S. oz.]

Henna (*Lawsonia inermis*)

PLATE 46:

Flowers of henna, along with those of saffron and hazelwort (which is used to make head-clearing snuff today), were thought to lull inebriated Romans into an untroubled slumber, dispersing the distempers and blunting the effects of intoxication.

> The scents of some flowers, as they disperse upward about the brain, clean out the conduits [*poroi*] of the organs of sense, and by their warmth thin and easily separate the humors without violence and shock. . . . (Plutarch, *Table Talk* III.i)

intoxication. (For the same reason, the image of an ivy bush was painted above tavern doors to pronounce on the quality of the wines sold within.) Other flowers would be wound into garlands hung around the neck, so that the warmer scents would gently ". . .open the body's ducts (*poroi*) and give the wine a vent; and those which are soothingly cool [thus, violets and roses] check the fumes by their temperate touch." (Plutarch, *Table Talk* III.I). Other plant garlands were worn at night, to inhibit the onset of hangovers during drunken slumber (Plate 46).

As has been the case throughout the centuries, however, many folk, once they were well intoxicated and free of inhibition, simply went whole hog, caring nothing about their likely state on the morrow and dropping all pretension of etiquette.

> Come, boy, you who serve out the old Falernian, fill up stronger cups for me, as the law of Postumia, mistress of the revels, ordains; Postumia more tipsy than the tipsy grape. But water, be gone, away with you—water, the destruction of wine—and take up your abode with scrupulous folk. . . . (Catullus, *Poems* XXVII)

And once the damage was done, they would seek out the proverbial "dog that bit them," and "go to accustomed haunts, thinking to expel and dispel wine with wine, and headache with headache." (Plutarch, *Table Talk*: Advice about Keeping Well.127). At that stage, who would argue with the wry comment of one Greek playwright, "If the headache only came to us before we drank to intoxication, no one would ever indulge himself in wine immoderately." (Athenaeus, *Banquet of the Philosophers* x.429, attributed to Alexis' *The Phrygian*)

I have yet to see the modern hangover cure of a raw egg or two promoted in ancient literature, though there certainly were plenty of notions of the kind in vogue at certain times. For example, a doctor who was close to the emperor Tiberius' son, Drusus, swore that the eating of a handful of bitter almonds before a party prevented him from getting drunk. To explain his immunity to intoxication, he invoked the empirical notion that, because the almonds were recognized for a cathartic property which could even remove facial pimples, then it was clear their bitterness irritated his body's pores. The wine's vapors then would be drawn away from his head before befuddlement could set in. The proof of the pudding about this, according to one convivium guest, was what happens to foxes: ". . .if they eat bitter almonds and drink nothing afterwards, they die of complete desiccation." (Plutarch, *Table Talk* I.6); notwithstanding that their feed was really rich in poisonous hydrocyanic acid.

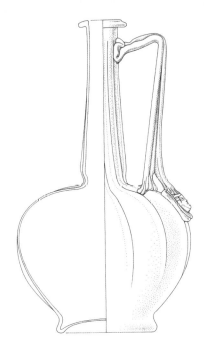

Nepos, my neighbor twice over, you have a daughter whose face is stamped with her father's likeness, witness to her mother's virtue. However, don't be too sparing of your aged Falernian; rather leave behind you jars full of cash. Let your girl be dutiful, let her be rich, but let her drink the new wine [when she grows up]; the flagon that is new now will grow old with its mistress. Let no Caecuban vintage nourish only the childless. Fathers too can enjoy life, take my word.

(Martial, *Epigrams* V.64)

Mold-blown, ribbed jug found in a grave
in Cologne, on the Rhine frontier
Late 1st century A.D.

XIII

THE WAYS OF THE WORLD

SUCH WAS THE RIGMAROLE SURROUNDING THE CON-
VIVIUM AND THE COMMISATIO OF THE WEALTHY. In the city taverns, poorer Romans enjoyed drinking games including the toasting of ladies, present or absent, according to their name—one measure of wine to be thrown down for each letter in it. Thus nine measures were drunk for VETUSTINA who was reputed to have buried two hundred husbands; and another nine measures for PROCULINA who was best known for having false-ly accused her husband of adultery so that she could be free to marry her own secret lover (see Martial, *Epigrams* III.93 and IV.22, respectively). Other times, the rhythm of the measures to be drunk was dictated by the roll of a die. Though the usual Roman measure of wine (a *cyathus*) was only close to one-six-teenth of the content of a modern French wine bottle, the rapidity of con-sumption and sheer amount of wine—almost certainly drunk undiluted during a game of this sort—made the evening a thoroughly rowdy one. Many a pick-pocket made his living off these revelers as they headed home across the silent squares and through the city's dark alleyways where even the peace-keeping *vig-iles* were loath to venture after dusk.

Interestingly though, the criticisms leveled at drunks of whatever social status was less for their excesses per se than for the fact that a hangover prevented the individual from taking full advantage of the daylight hours in pursuit of his business or his craft. A sleepy, befuddled head would not make money in the aggressive world of the Roman economy: ". . . whereas other men daily lose their yesterdays, these people lose their tomorrows also." (Pliny, *Natural History* XIV.143)

Alcoholics became the stuff of legends in the Classical World, just as authors such as Ernest Hemingway and pop idols such as Keith Richards of the Rolling Stones have done in recent years. Their seeming ability to carry on writing or performing without overt ill-effect gained them an odd public respect. As ever, most of our literary sources on such matters date to the latter half of the 1st century A.D. Thus, Pliny, with his typical attention to detail, devoted an entire section of Book XIV in his encyclopaedic *Natural History* to this topic, noting in particular how, during the reign of the emperor Tiberius (A.D. 14-37), a fashion developed for drinking on an empty stomach. He described at

length the lifestyle of one particular government official, Novellius Torquantus of Mediolanensis (modern Milan), who earned the surname of *Tricongius* (about 2.6 U.S. gallons), because of his ability to drain that measure of wine in one draught. Torquantus prided himself on never having stammered while he was drinking, or ever having relieved himself by vomiting or otherwise on such occasions, yet having always turned up for duty for the morning guard without anything going wrong. Such was the code of rules for him and those who tried to emulate his imbibing talent. Both the satirist Juvenal (*Satires* V.47) and historian Tacitus (*Annals* XV.34) tell of a character named Vatinius—a cobbler by trade and a sometime companion of the emperor Nero—whose drinking bouts were so notorious that a special wine glass was fashioned with four drinking spouts, each of which was said to match his similarly extended nose.

Several other Roman writers seem to have been seeking to fuel a strange kind of social controversy as to how these early imperial drunkards stacked up against their Greek peers in times long gone by. They could cite as sources the respected 4th century B.C. *Histories* of Theomompus, who

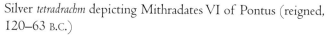

PLATE 47:

Silver *tetradrachm* depicting Mithradates VI of Pontus (reigned, 120–63 B.C.)

This king was nicknamed Dionysus, though apparently not out of recognition of his excessive drinking habits, but rather because of an incident that legend has it mirrored what happened to the wine-god himself at birth:

> Actually, when he was a baby, a bolt of lightning burned his swaddling clothes, but did not touch his body, except for a trace of the fire which remained on his forehead as a youth and was concealed by his hair. (Plutarch, *Table Talk* I.xi)

Mithridates had good reason to suspect that someone might poison his wine—during his tumultuous reign he survived by killing four of his sons—so he spent a lot of time searching for reliable antidotes (Majno 1975). The "prescription" that survived into Roman folklore was duly named *Mithridatium* and consisted of two dried walnuts, two figs, and twenty leaves of rue, plus a pinch of salt (see Pliny, *Natural History* XXIII.149).

provided an extensive list of drink-lovers and sots, and several works entitled *On Drunkenness*—sadly now only surviving in a few fragments of text—by the renowned philosophers, Aristotle and Theophrastus, among others. Thus, Plutarch (*Table Talk* I.xi) could describe at length the exploits of the boxer, Heraclides of Alexandria, who would invite different groups of guests to join him for drinks before lunch and during it, then for dinner and after it, reducing all of them in turn to a drunken stupor as he stumbled onward through the day. Athenaeus (*Banquet of the Philosophers* X.436) could write of Diotimus of Athens, who was nicknamed "Funnel" because he would drink wine unceasingly as it was poured into his mouth that way; and also of Xenarchus of Rhodes, who was nicknamed "Amphora-belly" because of his capacity for drink.

For such writers, alcoholism also was a valuable political tool for blackening, in hindsight, the reputation of several of Rome's more effective political and military enemies. An easy target was the Seleucid king Antiochus IV (reigned, 214-164 B.C.) who had sought to reconsolidate his Empire from Cilicia to Syria, only to run afoul of the eastward-expanding Romans when he tried to add Egypt and Cyprus to his domain. His drinking bouts were decried as an obvious sign of moral weakness. His critics could recall the words of the great historian, Polybius, who nicknamed the king Epimanes ["insane"] rather than his own choice of Epiphanes ["illustrious"], then recounted not only his drinking excesses but also his frequent bouts of bizarre behavior. The latter included an incident of pouring so much greasy scent on the head of a man in the marketplace that the surrounding crowd rolled head-over-heels in the mess (see Athenaeus, *Banquet of the Philosphers* x.439).

More harshly criticized still was Mithridates VI of Pontus, who was such a thorn in the side of the Romans as they expanded their territories eastward during the second-quarter of the 1st century B.C. He was reputed to have sponsored contests with prizes for the greatest eater and the greatest drinker, thereafter always winning those titles himself (Plate 47). Then, of course, Romans could take a swipe at the morality or strangeness of not just an individual but rather at an entire foreign culture that once had baulked at their military ambitions:

> They [the Persians] carry on their most important deliberations when drinking wine; and they regard decisions then made as more lasting than those they made when sober. (Strabo, *Geography* XV.3)

Fescennia, not wishing to reek of yesterday's wine, you greedily devour [the perfumer] Cosmus' pastilles. Such breakfasts smear the teeth, but they are no obstacle when a belch comes back from the depth of the abyss. Moreover, the evil element smells worse when mixed with scented powder and the doubled odor of the breath carries further. So away now with your too familiar tricks and detected cheats, and be a simple drunk.

(Martial, *Epigrams* I.87)

Detail from *A Merry Company at Table*, painted in 1630 by the Haarlem artist, Hendrick Pot

XIV

A SEPARATE STANDARD

THESE AND MANY OTHER STORIES OF LEGENDARY DRUNKARDS INDICATE WELL ENOUGH that throughout the centuries of Roman domination of the Mediterranean lands, it was a man's world. Business was a husband's prerogative; in all social classes, women from an early age were expected to assume the traditional role of child-bearer and child-rearer. A Roman man had a public identity—a goldsmith or a barber or a magistrate—whereas a woman had only her private life, defined by being someone's daughter, someone's wife, or someone's mother. A husband could obtain a divorce on various grounds—among them, a wife's infertility or adultery—whereas an official blind eye was turned on his indulgence in occasional sex with slaves or lower-class women. (The emperor Augustus, himself not exactly a paragon of virtue, only banished the poet Ovid from Rome because his *The Art of Love* was so blatant in its instruction on seduction and deception.) A husband could roll home drunk any time he wished and even expect some sympathy for the following morning's headache; a wife would be shamed for drinking in public, and even in private she would be expected to show moderation. Respectability did allow, however, for women to take a modicum of raisin wine (*passum*: see Plate 32).

Laurel (*Laurus nobilis*)

PLATE 48:

The oil of this plant has a distinctive fragrance that makes it a popular ingredient in perfumes and detergents today (Leung 1980); in fact, so distinctive that, even when mixed with wine, it lingers.

> Myrtale is apt to smell of much wine, but to fool us she devours laurel leaves and mixes her liquor with the canny foilage, not with water. Whenever, Paulus, you see her coming your way flushed, with her veins standing out, you may say: 'Myrtale has drunk laurel'. (Martial, *Epigrams* V.4)

In terms of Roman morality, adultery was a serious crime; so much so that there were provisions laid out in the emperor Augustus' *Julian Law* which gave a father or a husband the right to kill his daughter or his wife if the adulturous couple was caught *in flagrante*. (If a husband did not exert that right, he had no choice but to divorce his wife, or else find himself liable for punishment as a pimp.) Frequently in real life, adultery and drunkenness went hand-in-hand; a wife's intoxication often was sound reason for at least severe censure and sometimes for something far worse.

> Egnatius Mecenius beat his wife to death with a club because she had drunk some wine. And not only did no one bring him to court because of his deed, but no one even reproached him, for all the best men thought that she deserved the punishment for her example of intemperance. For assuredly any woman who desires to drink immoderately closes the door to all virtues and opens it to all vices. (Valerius Maximus, *Memorable Deeds and Words* VI.3.9)

It was quite hard for a woman to hide her alcoholism—distracting scents most times simply did not work (Plate 48); and if the cravings became too intense to bear, the consequences could be dire. For example, Pliny (*Natural History* XIV.89) recounted the story of a matron who was starved to death by her relatives for having broken open the casket containing the keys to the wine cellar.[47]

In these circumstances, as one might imagine, past "heroines" to match the likes of the plebian Heraclides or the regal Mithridates were few and far between. One of the attendees of Athenaeus' *Banquet of the Philosophers* was able to keep the conversation going with the recollection of a certain Cleo who, in the 4th century B.C., offered her saffron tunic to a gold image of Dionysus, in recognition of how she excelled at the symposia she attended. Beyond that, however, historical record thankfully spares us the notion of a female "Amphora-belly."

Women, with the notable exception of Cleopatra, never held the reins of power in the Classical World, at least overtly. (What we know of Livia's influence upon the emperor Augustus and of Agrippina's role in gaining imperial authority for her teenage son Nero makes that last qualifying phrase quite essential.) So there was rarely a political need, in historical hindsight, to besmerch the reputation of powerful women. Lurid reports of debauchery in general, and sexual debauchery in particular, were the preferred attack weapon.[48]

So it was with the criticism made by the early 2nd century A.D. historian, Cornelius Tacitus, against the emperor Claudius' third wife, Valeria Messallina. In Book XI of his *Annals*, he writes with near-voyeuristic fascination of Claudius' blindness to the course and purpose of that lady's adulteries; even observing how, by A.D. 48, such behavior had become so easy for Messallina that "she was drifting towards untried [unspecified] debaucheries." Yet drunkenness never figures directly in the charges against her. Only when she was so politically provocative as to proceed with an illegal marriage ceremony with her current lover, the consul-designate, Gauis Silius, does wine enter the record:

> Autumn was at the full, and she was celebrating a mimic vintage through the grounds of the house. Presses were being trodden, vats flowed; while besides them skin-girt women were bounding like Bacchanals excited by sacrifice or delirium. She herself was there with dishevelled tresses and waving *thyrsus*; at her side, Silius [impersonated Bacchus] with a ivy crown, wearing the buskins and tossing his head, while around him rose the din of a wanton chorus. (Tacitus, *Annals* XI.xxxi)

Whether Claudius, who was in Ostia at the time, ever learned of this wild party, we don't know: in other circumstances, the event might have appealed to him since he is known to have drunk well and often. It was the tales brought to him of Silius' improper nuptial bed that brought forth his fury and a call for the executioner.

The male Roman attitude towards women drinking created some significant social tensions. The convivium for the most part was structured around the family and a circle of friends. Yet many Roman moralists felt that if the men and women present drank on a par with one another, thoughts would surely turn to adultery. A Christian philosopher explained the chemistry of this process quite simply: "The eating of meat and the drinking of wine and the fullness of the stomach is the seed plot of lust." (St. Jerome, *Against Jovinianus* II.7).

Such an attitude might imply that the Romans thought that women were more liable to intoxication than men, more prone to let inebriation loosen their morals. Yet, many an ancient writer presented reasoned "medical" explanations that the very opposite was true. Thus, one guest at Plutarch's *convivium* noted how women possessed a moist temperament which was responsible for their delicate, smooth skin. This natural moisture would heavily dilute the wine and so make it lose its edge.[49] Rationale here came through comparison to the way that old men responded to wine quite differently—reputedly with trembling limbs, irascibility, and a wandering mind—all signs that apparently were due to a dryness of substance which would soak up wine like a sponge, keeping it locked and heavy within the body—thus, the wonderful observation: "Nothing is more like an old man than a young man drunk." (Plutarch, *Table Talk* III.650).

It is intriguing how much such Roman notions are at odds with modern medical opinion, which reckons that a woman's body contains less water (relative to fat) so that the blood alcohol concentration (BAC) will increase more rapidly in her tissues than in those of a man of equal weight. (Heavier men can tolerate higher BAC-levels.) At the same time, we now know that the enzyme, Alcohol Dehydrogenase (ADH), which is involved in the metabolism of alcohol within the body, has a lower activity in women, so that they become drunk significantly more rapidly than their male counterparts.[50] The Roman view on these matters appears to be quite intentionally misleading; for what purpose, who can say?

Opium poppy (*Papaver somniferum*)

Food and drink are useful not only to cure every type of disease, but also to guarantee good health. Therefore it is necessary to understand their properties, so that healthy people know how to use them, and that in the event of illness one knows which should be consumed.

(Celsus, *On Medicine* II.18)

XV

THE MEDICINALS

THUS FAR I HAVE FOCUSED ON THE MORE FAMILIAR ASPECTS OF WINE CONSUMPTION—the pleasure of drinking it on its own merits if the vintage quality is good; and as an adjunct to various kinds of food, in which instance it sometimes would bring out extra piquancy in the dish being served or just subtly complement the food, whether it was a strongly flavored fish, a well-spiced meat, or an egg-rich dessert. But, of course, there were other uses of wine in the Roman World. We don't have to stray far from earlier themes to note here how often wine was a common ingredient in the variety of sauces that were prepared to accompany a supper's main course (Plate 49).[51] Still within the realms of Roman culinary interests, we should recognize the significant place of sour wine or vinegar as a preservative for all manner of staple foodstuffs and culinary herbs, such as turnips, green olives, capers, parsley, samphire, butcher's broom—as a salad alternative to asparagus—and the ever popular and versatile fennel (Plate 50). Without such a preservative, much of the produce of the Campanian countryside would never have reached or survived in the city of Rome long enough to attract the praise of the early Imperial gourmets and satirists.[52] Both wine and its by-product vinegar, however, in addition to their many uses with food, had a completely different and really quite important role in Roman medicine.

The Romans followed the Greeks in the belief that the cause of disease was an imbalance among the body's four humors: blood, phlegm, yellow bile, and black bile. Wellness meant that the humors were in harmony; sickness implied a disharmony in the humors' blend, with phlegm and bile considered the usual

PLATE 49:

A SAUCE FOR SERVING SEASONED LENTILS WITH WILD ARTICHOKES
From Apicius' *De Re Coquinaria*: recipe 183 (after Giacosa 1992)
Ingredients: 1 Tbs. of mixed herbs (such as cumin, coriander seeds, mint, rue, and pennyroyal), 1 Tbs. of vinegar, 1 tsp. each of honey and *garum*, and 1Tbs. of *defrutum*.
Preparation: The ingredients are simply mixed together, then added to the lentils which have previously been boiled and drained.
Besides being used in sauces for both vegetable and meat dishes, *defrutum* also was recommended as a preservative for bottled quinces and mulberries (see Apicius' recipes 20 and 23, respectively).

PLATE 50:

The unopened flower and stalk of this and other popular culinary herbs, such as black lovage, capers, and rue, would be preserved in a mixture of two-parts vinegar to one-part brine (see Columella, *On Agriculture* XII.vi and XII.lvii). Taken out and dried just a few sprigs at a time, fennel was a flavorsome garnish for many a Roman fish dish.

Fennel (*Foeniculum vulgare*)

PLATE 51:

Wine steeped in the fruit juices of this plant, along with scammony (*Convulvulus scammonia*) and the two hellebores (white *Veratrum album* and black *Helleborus niger*), was one of the harshest of Roman medicinals, being an intense purgative (Riddle 1985). It usually was used to treat kidney complaints. This plant's tendency to vary in toxicity from season to season made it a risky substance to ingest, though its ability to stimulate one of the humors, yellow bile, enhanced its stature among Roman doctors (Stuart 1979).

Squirting cucumber (*Ecballium elaterium*)

PLATE 52:

THE TREATMENT OF *IGNI SACRO*

Ingi sacro is treated with aizoüm, pounded leaves of hemlock, and root of mandrake—it is cut into slices as is cucumber, hung first over must, then in smoke, and finally pounded—taken in wine or vinegar. It is beneficial to foment with myrtle wine, or to use as an ointment two ounces of mint with one ounce of native sulphur beaten up together in vinegar, or soot mixed with vinegar. There are several kinds of *igni sacro*, among them one called *zoster*, which goes round the patient's waist, and is fatal if the circle becomes quite complete. Remedies are plantain with Cimolian chalk, peristereos by itself, and the root of persollata; as remedies for the creeping forms can be used root of cotyledon with *mulsum* [honey wine], aizoüm, and the juice of linozostis with vinegar. (Pliny, *Natural History* XXVI.121)

Among Roman physicians, *igni sacro* seems to have a quite broad medical term, equating to some form of eczema or lupus, or in the case of the disease *zoster* mentioned here, a rash due to shingles.

Of the other less common plantstuffs in this recipe:

aizoüm	stonecrop (*Sedum album*)
peristereos	vervain (*Verbena officianalis*)
persollata	common dock (*Aretium lappa*)
cotyledon	navelwort (*Cotyledon umbilicus*)
linozostis	white horehound (*Marrubium vulgare*) (see Plate 56)

culprits. Food, though a necessity, was regarded as a primary source of disease, because inadequate digestion could result in the build-up of harmful residues within the body. So a logical course of treatment would be: (i) bleeding, to get rid of the excess of a misbehaving humor; (ii) starvation, to prevent the troubling humor from re-establishing itself; and (iii) purging, to remove any possible residual bad humors still lurking somewhere in the body. The last of these assaults on the disease was not regarded as some kind of tidying-up of the problem; some of the common Roman purgatives were extremely powerful, bordering on the lethal (Plate 51). As the ancient philosophers sought to define the fundamentals of our existence, the notion of four-fold symmetry extended to the material qualities—hot, cold, dry, and moist—that delicately fuse to define human temperament and its individual variability.[53]

Within this framework, wine was characterized as cold. Medicinally, it was placed a notch below narcotics such as mandrake and opium, which were ultra-cold in the sense that they reduced the patient's fever and quite abruptly induced a state of torpor. By contrast, wine dulled the senses gradually and, some would argue, in a far more pleasant way. By a similar token, wine's coldness would inspire drunken sleep by overwhelming the human body's natural heat, and it would induce sexual inadequacy by chilling the burning energy of love-making. At a convivium, no one would debate the observation: ". . .old men certainly have a cold nature, and drunkards especially resemble old men." (Plutarch, *Table Talk* III.652): in the Classical World that would have come under the heading of "common knowledge."

A doctor's patients might come from all walks of life; on one day, there might be a professional boxer, his eyes bloated and blackened in contests; on another, a shopkeeper's wife complaining of a stubborn ankle ulcer caused by her varicose veins. In the poorer area of a city, a slave might seek treatment for a back lacerated by a whipping. If some of the sores had become inflamed by infection, the doctor might cover them with a paste composed of the juice of wild celery—a plant much respected for its "coldness"—some crushed garlic and/or some cheap wine, both of which for centuries past had been recognized for their antiseptic properties.[54] Then, in best Hippocratic tradition, the slave inevitably would be given a purge—perhaps a concoction of sour wine and juice boiled out of the foliage of Alexandrian senna.

The Classical theory of humors even spilled

PLATE 53:

This plant gained a reputation in the ancient world for its contraceptive properties, the flowering plant being concocted into a tea for that purpose (Riddle 1997; Scarborough 1996). In higher doses, however, it causes irritation to the genito-urinary tract that result in reflex uterine contractions that could be sufficiently strong to induce abortion.

Pennyroyal (*Mentha pulegium*) from Dioscorides' *De Materia Medica*

There is also a third kind of *phalangium*, a hairy spider with an enormous head. When this is cut open, there are said to be found inside two little worms, which, tied in deer skin as an amulet on women before sunrise, act as a contraceptive. . .Of all such preventives this only would it be right for me to mention, to help those women who are so prolific that they stand in need of such a respite. (Pliny, *Natural History* XXIX.85)

Albeit that his notions of contraception have little medical substance, perhaps Pliny's heart was in the right place. Roman women married in their teens and were expected to bear one child after another from then on. Each childbirth carried with it a real risk of not just the death of the baby but of the mother as well. Roman midwives were respected for their experience with herbs such as rue that allowed control of menstruation, and ones such as mandrake that could ease labor pains (see Plate 54). They knew the herbal abortives just as well; plantstuffs that could be found stored in any Roman kitchen—leaves of pennyroyal that would be burned to repel insects and the pungent herb, asafetida (called *silphium* or *laserpitium* in antiquity, depending upon where it came from) that was used in so many sauces for meat.

The leaves of *silphium* are used in medicine to purge the uterus and to bring away the dead unborn baby; a decoction of them made in white, aromatic wine, to be drunk after the bath in doses of one *acetabalum*. (Pliny, *Natural History* XXII.100)

over to the treatment of external problems such as bruises, swellings, and almost any kind of skin rash (Plate 52); to a Roman's way of thinking, these were an outward manifestation of a disharmony in the underlying mix of humors. Poultices would be needed then, and in the Roman pharmacopaea there were dozens of them, such as one made up from dried rootstock of black bryony that could have been used on the contusions of the battered boxer mentioned earlier; and one based on the juices extracted from hemlock that was said to be effective against breast tumors. Each of these medicinals most likely was mixed into a paste with some wine, again to take advantage of its antiseptic powers.

Perhaps wine's most common role in Roman medicine, however, was as a vehicle with a pleasing taste that could offset or mask the intense bitterness of something like a purge based on aloe or a diuretic prepared from the roots of sorrel. (Anyone today who mistakenly bites into the caplet of some antibiotic or laxative would understand that usage well enough, though the bottle it came from is more likely now to bear a label warning *against* taking the medicine with alcohol.) The mind-numbing powers of wine, in excess, also may have made more tolerable a women's decision to induce abortion with a common herb such as rue or pennyroyal (Plate 53), or with something more violent-acting but assuredly effective as scammony or black hellebore.[55] She may have preferred that approach to the very real risks of infection during careless surgery, or to the rigors of home-spun solutions such as being expected to make violent leaps in the air or being shaken about while astride a draught animal before being heavily "bled" (see Soranus of Ephesus, *Gynaeocology* I.64).

Quackery was rife in the world of Roman medicine so anyone purporting to be a professional doctor was often regarded with some suspicion—thus the witticisms: "Dialus was once a surgeon, now he is an undertaker. He's started to practice medicine the only way he knew how." (Martial, *Epigrams* I.30); and "You are a gladiator now, you were formerly an eye doctor. You did as a doctor what you do as a gladiator." (Martial, *Epigrams* VIII.74). Since there were no formal requirements for entering the medical profession, such cynicism may well have had some basis. Often the "training" of a doctor amounted to no more than following one of his colleagues about, each sharing empirical experiences

with one other until some consensus of medical knowledge emerged.

Many competent doctors surely did emerge from such a "hands-on" and colleagial approach to learning. Still, a lot of folk preferred to try and cure themselves, whenever possible, buying bunches of medicinal herbs at the local marketplace, and storing them till needed. A timely concoction of extract of hyssop in some honeyed wine might work well against bronchitis; leaves of bear's breech soaked in vinegar might ease the pain of an unexpected scald; flower heads of vervain in some *passum* might calm a housewife's nerves; and so on. All these home cures just might work, without a doctor, skilled or otherwise, ever coming near the house.

While lay folk might, over the years, share folk-lore with their neighbors and build up an extensive stock of herbal medicines—many of which would double as cosmetic or culinary ingredients, or vice-versa[56]—at the frontier forts and briefly settled encampments of the Empire, the luxury of time often was in short supply. For centuries, a mix of skirmishes and flat-out wars was a way-of-life in the outlying parts of many of the provinces, and legionary medics were for ever busy salving burns and trying to staunch bloody wounds. Meanwhile surgeons struggled to save torn and pusridden limbs that were threatened by gangrene and the like. The anaesthetics of the day were wine-soaked narcotics such as henbane, opium, and mandrake (Plate 54).

Even when a frontier was relatively quiet, it was

Mandrake (*Mandragora officinarum*)

PLATE 54:

The juices produced by boiling down the root of this plant provided one of the most powerful pain-killers available in ancient times. Roman surgeons used heavy doses of it to sedate their patients, while Roman doctors would mix it with rose oil and wine to treat eye problems and snake-bites. Such was its strength, ". . .some find it enough to put themselves to sleep by the smell. A dose of two *oboli* of mandrake is also taken in honey wine instead of hellebore. . .as an emetic and to purge away black bile." (Pliny, *Natural History* XXV.149). It was a drug that could easily be stored, its root being cut into round slices and preserved in wine until needed (see Plate 52).
Mandrake wine also was used for the relief of toothache, though with due caution: "The patient should carefully avoid swallowing the fluid in the mouth." (Celsus, *On Medicine* VI.9)

rarely all that pleasant a place to be. A military hospital in the northwestern provinces, for example, would certainly be stocked with surgical instruments, common antiseptic ointments, and lots of jars crammed with local herbs, such as vitamin-rich dock that would relieve scurvy and obstinate skin complaints, and plantain that would help heal abscesses and ease hacking coughs. There also would be numerous concoctions that might deal with the savagery of snake and insect bites of a kind that most city folk preferred to remain oblivious; and, in storage, there would be several amphorae packed full with essential wine-preserved herbs for all sorts of diseases associated with the

rigors and deprivations of army life.[57] Many of these herbs, like some of the preserved foodstuffs mentioned earlier, may have been carted in from quite far afield. Yet these were the staples of the everyday treatment of soldiers faced with the bitter winter cold of the Rhineland or the burning heat of Eastern deserts—fenugreek mixed with fig juice for pneumonia, St. John's wort for blistered and burnt skin, and so on (Plates 55 and 56). A soldier might dream of spending his veteran years sipping myrrh-flavored Falernian; until that time came, and while he remained in the combat zone, he would needs accept a horehound-flavored vinegar.

PLATE 55:

Seeds of this very bitter-tasting herb were found in abundance during excavation of the hospital quarter (*valetudinarium*) at the 1st century A.D. legionary fort of Novaesium (modern Neuss) on the Rhine (Davies 1970). It was recommended in ancient texts for healing wounds, curing eye ailments, and when mixed with wine, as an antidote to snake bites.

Centaury (*Centaurium umbrellatum*)

White horehound (*Marrubium vulgare*) from Dioscorides' *De Materia Medica*

PLATE 56:

Graffiti on the shoulder of an amphora found at Carpow—a early 2nd century A.D. fort which lay about a hundred miles north of Hadrian's Wall—indicates that this bitter-tasting plant was mixed with wine to treat bronchitis and coughs among the soldiers stationed there (Jackson 1988). It also was used in the treatment of shingles (see Plate 52).

Detail from a funerary chest from Ephesus which contained
the cremated remains of the soldier, Titus Valerius Secundus
1st century A.D.

I should like to have all kinds of
fruit growing around my ashes, and
plenty of vines. It is quite wrong
for a man to decorate his house
while he is alive, and not trouble
about the house where he must
make a longer stay.

(Petronius, *Satyricon*. 71)

XVI

RELIGIOUS OVERTONES

EARLY IN THIS BOOK (SEE II: MARKETS OLD AND NEW) I COMMENTED THAT THE ROMANS really had little confidence in their own potential as vintners until 121 B.C., the "Opimian" year; until then, imported Greek wines held sway in the Italian wine market. There can be little doubt, however, that the Romans would have persevered for as along as necessary to become masters of the grape. Such determination was the hallmark of the Romans dogged rise to power over the Mediterranean region, and of their sponge-like absorption of foreign ideas and knowledge, whether technical skills that enhanced efficiency of craft production or abstract philosophies that would influence the tempo of everyday life. It was enslavement of experienced workmen from among the conquered peoples—pottery-makers from Asia Minor and glass-workers from Syria and Judaea, most obviously, but also skilled farmhands from all of Rome's territories—that underpinned Roman technological success. It was the influx of foreign peoples into the Italian peninsula, and particularly into Rome itself, that so dramatically changed the complexion of Roman society time and again over the centuries. The Roman fascination with, and appreciation of, foreign ideas assured the success of many oriental cults during the Republican era, not least that of the Greek wine-god, Dionysus, whom the Romans would transform into Bacchus (Plate 57).

79

PLATE 57:

This mid 1st century B.C. wall-painting from a burial niche in the Villa Pamphili in Rome captures the various aspects of Bacchic revelry that so concerned the pious Republican Romans—the god himself inciting his followers with his phallus openly displayed, the naked, ecstatic maenad, and the two constant companions of Bacchus, the pipe-playing Pan and the drunken Silenus. The event would be complete if there were a few more maenads adding to its raucousness with the clatter of cymbals. The noisiness of these *bacchanalia* not only was irritating for many folk but also was regarded with suspicion by them.

> And [there occurred] poisonings and murders too, so secret that sometimes the bodies were not even located for burial. . .The violence was concealed, however, because the shrieks of these tortured by deviant sex or murder could not be heard above the loud wails and the crash of drums and cymbals.
> (Livy, *A History of Rome* XXXIX.14)

The long history of development of Bacchic rituals in Greece from the 8th century B.C. onward is well summarized in Johnson (1989) and Lambert-Gócs (1990).

The initial intrusion of Dionysic ideas into Roman culture probably occurred during the early 3rd century B.C., as Rome took control of the areas of southern Italy which had been colonized by Greek farmers some three hundred years earlier. Its initial presence is now imperceptible: perhaps it was sustained only by word-of-mouth description among Rome's slave population. (It may well have gained some extra impetus by virtue of the fact that Rome's northern neighbors in Etruria had blended Dionysus and their own similarly attributed Fufluns into a single deity, and were openly promoting the cult's virtues.) Ancient texts do indicate clearly enough, however, that by 186 B.C. the Bacchic cult had gained sufficient popularity to be regarded as a threat to the stability of the State. It was then that an official purge was ordered.

In the eyes of the Roman Senate, the beliefs of the cult itself were only part of the problem. The core value of early Roman religious practices was piety—an upright way of life, coupled with constant attention to all rituals that ensured peace of mind among the ancestors; this was key to Roman preparation for the Afterlife. The possibility of a personal redemption through mystery-laden communion with the divine powers, whether it was with the god Bacchus, or indeed with any of the cultic figures of the day, such as the Egyptian goddess Isis or the Phrygian goddess Cybele, ran counter to traditional pagan values and threatened customary patterns of Roman worship. So any circulation of such unusual ideas among the general citizenry was most worrisome, as were rumors of mysterious Bacchic rites which were emotional to the point of frenzy and, it was said, prone to lewdness and drunken devilry.

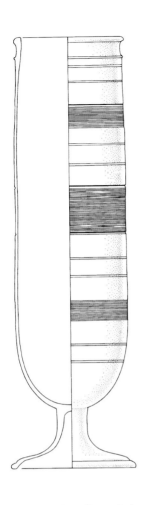

PLATE 58:

Colorless, heavily engraved glass flute (Ht., 13.7 inches) from a tomb at Sedeinga just south of the Third Cataract on the Nile in Egypt
With this flute was found an almost identical, but larger one, and two others painted and gilded with scenes of offerings to the Egyptian deity, Osiris. There are some signs that all this glassware was ritually smashed for some reason at the time of the tomb's closure (Leclant 1973).
The quality and composition of the flute indicates that it most likely was made in Alexandria around A.D. 280. Its appreciable capacity—almost 2.5 Roman *sextarii* [2.8 U.S. pints or 1.33 liters]—surely puts it out of the realm of typical tableware. One has to imagine that the wine it held was shared during a funerary custom of some importance.

When the wine had enflamed their minds, and the dark night and the intermingling of men and women, young and old, had smothered every feeling of modesty, depravities of every kind began to take place because each person had ready access to whatever perversion his mind was inclined. There is not just one kind of immorality, not just promiscuous and deviant sex between freeborn men and women, but false witnesses and forged seals, wills, and documents of evidence also issued from this same 'office'. (Livy, *A History of Rome* XXXIX.14)

In truth, then, at the heart of Roman discomfort with the Bacchic cult was the way it was organized as cells with leadership which demanded oaths of loyalty and a say in the dispersal of property and inheritance. So the cult was labeled as a *superstitio*—translating as "irresponsible" here—and the target of the Senate decree was more its leadership than the reputed orgiastic behavior of its followers. As a consequence, about 7000 people from all over Italy were accused of conspiracy against the State. I assume that most of these were put to death for their beliefs.

Savage though this and several later persecutions were, the Bacchic cult not only survived but flourished off-and-on through the years. By the mid 1st century B.C., it had shaken free of its roots as a faith for the common man and was finding adherents among Rome's wealthy and powerful. The latter pressured Julius Caesar to lift the ban on Bacchic festivals. For centuries thereafter their festivals were one of the many annual street celebrations which entertained and amused the city's citizenry with the somewhat bizarre antics and unabashed bent towards pleasure. The cult's favorite symbols—the meandering vine and the mask of revelry—became a decorative feature of many a Roman sculptural relief, floor mosaic, and wine beaker all the way through till the late 4th century A.D. The cult

PLATE 59:

This kind of massive glass jar (Ht., 8.4 inches) first appeared in the Roman World in the mid 1st century A.D., initially being used as a household storage vessel for grain, pickled fish, preserved olives, etc. Soon it was finding secondary usage—along with grain measures, large wine bottles and discarded amphorae—as an urn to hold someone's cremated remains. In burial it most likely was given some protection by being placed inside another container made of pottery or lead sheeting (Fleming 1997).

Many of these urns were provided with a new lid; one with a hole pierced through it and inverted so that it could serve as funnel. The burial then was linked to the surface above by a lead pipe (see INSET), or via the mouth of the pottery amphora which served as a grave marker in some of the more densely packed cemeteries near Rome. By this arrangement, the deceased could receive an offering of wine as part of the graveside meal (*cena novendialis*) which marked the end of the period of full mourning, and at many remembrance ceremonies which were included in the formal Roman calendar.

INSET

A reconstruction of how wine was ritually fed to the deceased, based on the layout of a late 1st century A.D. burial excavated at Carthage in north Africa (Barette (1989).

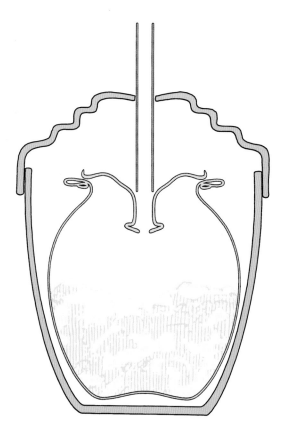

dwindled into insignificance thereafter, in part because of the emperor Constantine's adoption of Christianity as the State religion around A.D. 330 [58]; in part because so many aspects of Bacchic symbolism—not least the communal imbibing of wine as the blood of the deity—were subtly assimulated into the framework of Christian thought and art.[59]

In the story of Roman wine, therefore, the cult of Bacchus holds a special place—to the god's followers, wine was absolutely central to his worship. But wine was important for other cults too (Plate 58), and it played significant and specific roles within the rituals of mainstream Roman paganism as well. With the psyche of every Republican Roman rooted in the soil of Italy, wine and fertility rituals inevitably hung together early on.

Afterward offer wine to Janus with the following words: 'Father Janus, just as I humbly prayed when I offered you the sac-

rificial [wheat] crackers, so now for the same purpose be honored with sacrificial wine'. (Cato, *On Agriculture* CXXXIV)

Even the appreciable changes wrought in those rituals by the later adoption of so many foreign deities never broke that connection.

Through the latter part the 1st century B.C. and into the early part 2nd century A.D. when cremation was the norm for disposal of the deceased, every funeral was brought to a close by the simple act of dousing the flames of the pyre with wine. In the ceremonies which followed that cremation—not just the ones at the graveside that related directly to the interment of the remains, but also those that were held every year in honor of the ancestors—it was wine that was ritually shared by the living and the dead (Plate 59).

Meanwhile, when the family and relatives could afford to do so, the deceased's funerary urn—or the deceased's body itself, when cremation went out

PLATE 60:

Glass jug (Ht., 7.6 inches) with a reeded strap handle, dating to the late 4th century A.D. Back at the turn of the 3rd century A.D., when the pope Zephyrinus required that glassware be accepted for use among the ritual vessels for the Mass, he was probably formalizing the status quo for that ceremony thereafter, wherein glass bowls, flasks, and jugs like this one were part of the equipment of makeshift altars in households throughout the Empire. In many respects, their eventual use as grave goods continued that function (Fleming 1999).

of fashion in the mid-2nd century A.D.—would be accompanied in the grave by many of the essentials of everyday Roman life. Along with money, perfumed lotions, jewelry, and household implements, there would be platters of food and a cluster of beakers and wine-filled flasks (Plate 60). We can be sure that the wine itself befitted the social status of the deceased's family; or maybe it was pretentiously a little better than that they might drink themselves, since in Roman society the perception of wealth was sometimes more important than the reality.

These funerary rights must have changed quite dramatically in the mid 4th century A.D. as Christianity gained ascendency as the State religion. In life, a Christian was taught that he/she would have no use for earthly possessions in the blessed Hereafter. But many converts simply fitted certain traditional pagan notions, such as grave-side banquetry and a sharing of wine with the deceased, straight into their own understanding of the rituals of their new belief, even when those notions ran counter to the Gospels. This caused some dismay among Church leaders, but they could not ignore the speed at which their "flock" was growing at the cost of traditional paganism and rival cults. So high-minded consternation yielded to a mixture of paternal tolerance and personal soul-searching.

Their naivity is unconscious of the extent of their guilt, and their sins are from devotion, for they wrongly believe that their saints are delighted to have their tombs doused with reeking wine. . .But how can the saints approve after death what they condemned in their teaching? Does Peter admit to his table what his doctrine rejects? (Paulinus of Nola, *Poems* XVIII.566)

If I am right that the diet of many Roman babies included some wine consumption, both to shield them from the risks of drinking urban-piped water and at times to help them sleep, then wine played a part in every age of a Roman's life— through the excesses of youth and the more measured consumption of middle age, even unto death. Throughout those times, the wine carried with it a religious blessing that, in one way or another, watched over the Roman soul.

Let there be chosen from the brotherhood as Cellarer of the monastery a wise man, of settled habits, temperate and frugal, not conceited, irritable, resentful, sluggish, or wasteful, but fearing God, who may be as a father to the whole brotherhood.

(The Rule of St. Benedict XXI)

"The sleeve of Hippocrates": detail from the 15th century codex, *Tractatus de Herbis*.

XVII

EPILOGUE

IN SEPTEMBER A.D. 476, THE 16-YEAR-OLD ROMULUS AUGUSTULUS ABDICATED THE IMPERIAL OFFICE and retired to the Bay of Naples; historians did not even bother to record when he died. This seemingly quiet end to the Roman Empire in the West is deceptive, however. During the previous twenty years, following the assassination of emperor Valentinan III in A.D. 455, there had been eight emperors of varying degree of legitimacy. All of them were short-lived, and most of them were victim to murder based on political expediency. As each tried to consolidate the position through alliance with one Germanic tribe or another, northern Italy and the erstwhile Roman provinces in northwestern Europe became a war zone where the success of individual leaders flowed and ebbed like the tide.

As we have seen, during the 3rd century A.D. conflicts in Gaul that pitted the likes of the invading Franks and Alemanni against incumbent Roman garrisons, the lands given over to viticulture were, for the most part, damaged only by clod-footed carelessness and frightened farmers' neglect. The barbarian invaders prized the wines that previously they had bought in the marketplaces of Augusta Treverorum (modern Trier). So, when they had extended control over these lands, they encouraged the re-planting of local vineyards.

PLATE 61:

Gold coin (*solidus*) depicting king Gundobad in the early 6th century A.D. In A.D. 500 the Frankish king Clovis marched upon Dijon, set to do battle with the brothers Gundobad and Godigisel. The latter joined forces with Clovis, however, and Gundobad fled across the Rhône to Avignon. One of Gundobad's advisors hatched a plot, by which he, Aridius, first would claim to have changed allegiance as well. Having gained Clovis' confidence, he then would plead for his prince's life to be spared.

> You lay waste to the fields and devour the meadows, you cut the vines, you hew down the olives, all the fruits of this region you utterly destroy; and yet you do not prevail over him. Instead, send envoys to him and impose a yearly tribute that the region may be saved from ruin. . . . (Gregory of Tours, *History of the Franks* II.23)

But this was treachery too; when Gundobad recovered his strength, he refused to pay the tribute, re-grouped his army and besieged Godigisel at Vienne. Within weeks, Godigesel's forces were starved into submission, Godigesel himself was banished to Tolouse, and Gundobad once more held sway over the region of Burgundy.

In the century after Romulus Augustus' fall from power, however, the conflicts were far more mean-spirited, often setting kinsfolk against one another (Plate 61). For example, in a commentary for the year A.D. 583, on the activities of the dukes Desiderius and Bladast, who were acting on behalf of prince Chilperic (whom, because of his evil ways, some have characterized as a Frankish clone of Nero), we learn: "There remained not a house, nor a vineyard, nor a tree; all was cut down and ruined." (Gregory of Tours, *History of the Franks* VI.22).

A year later is was the turn of the Duke Bobo and his cronies, acting on behalf of king Childebert, to bring fresh misery to the life of the Gallic peasantry, thus: "They pillaged the cottages of the poor, ruined the vineyards by cutting off the vine-stems with the grapes still upon them, drove of the herds and seized everything within their reach." (Gregory of Tours, *History of the Franks* VII.32). And in A.D. 585, when Chilperic's brother, the king Guntrum, dispatched his forces to cut a swathe across Gaul, the citizenry of Nimes could only stand and watch from behind the safety of their city's mighty walls, as surrounding houses were fire-gutted, and olive groves and vineyards were hacked to shreds.

Time and again, vine cuttings were set only to be torn from the ground or burned as soon as they achieved some degree of maturity; livelihoods were intentionally crippled to the point where, towards the end of 6th century A.D., any report on the state of vine crops became a yardstick for how disastrous matters had become.[60]

Echoes from the Roman early Imperial era reverberate through this new European scene, as we read of an encounter between Queen Fredegund and a Frankish chief from Rouen:

> She then begged that, if he would not eat at her table, he would at least drink a cup and not go fasting from the royal dwelling. He waited, and they brought a cup from which he drank wormwood mixed with wine and honey, after the manner of the barbarians [Franks]. But the draught was poisoned, and no sooner had he drunk it than he felt great pain rise in his breast, as if he had been all cut within. (Gregory of Tours, *History of the Franks* VIII.31)

PLATE 62:

A gold *solidus* minted at Dorestadt and depicting Charlemagne sometime just before A.D. 800
The impact of this emperor on European viticulture bordered on the revolutionary. He tried to lay down strict laws about hygiene in wine-making, including the notion that the grapes should not be trodden with the feet, but no one then knew of any other way to extract the best juices. He banned the storage of wine in animal skins, to avoid spoilage—something that American vintners only came to realize as advisable a millennium later—and he opened up the marketing of wine by allowing vintners to hang out a green branch if they wanted to sell their produce on the spot (Johnson 1989).

Thereupon the unsuspecting guest was struck by blindness. Though he managed to mount his horse and flee the Queen's presence, he had ridden scarcely a third of a mile before he fell from his saddle and died.

With all this deceit and death hanging over the Gallic economy, the Western Mediterranean wine trade began to falter. People looked to the potential of their own lands for viticulture or enviously eyed the fertile soils of their neighbors. As the political turmoil stretched onwards through the 7th century A.D., the non-Christian Gascons of southwestern France were emboldened to join the fray. They surged forth from the Pyrenees into the plains of the Garrone and Dordogne rivers, there ravaging the fields and, of course, the vineyards, burning the houses and carrying off many farmers with their flocks and herds (see Gregory of Tours, *History of the Franks* IX.7). Try as they might, the Franks could not dislodge them; by the latter part of the 10th century A.D. the Gascons held Bordeaux, and they thrived on being able to trade much of their surplus wine stocks to England.

At this point, I have advanced far beyond the main topic and title of this book. The twists and turns in the story of European wine production from the period of Gascon expansion until today

are covered in detail by several excellent, readily available books, most notably Hugh Johnson's historically sweeping *Vintage: The Story of Wine*, and Jancis Robinson's encyclopaedic *The Oxford Companion to Wine*. There are a few aspects of Medieval wine-making that do deserve mention here, however, in that they display a heritage drawn from Roman times.

This heritage is nowhere more obvious than the role the Christian Church played in European viticulture. Many of the early bishops have a legendary connection with wine-making, starting with St. Martin who, after he became Bishop of Tours in A.D. 371, initiated vine cultivation in Touraine. A later bishop of Tours, St. Gregory, also was a great patron of the vine; another St. Gregory, this one the bishop of Langres, was not content with the wine yield of his episcopal lands and moved his seat to Dijon, in the heartland of burgundy country; and St. Ermelund planted a massive vineyard near the mouth of the Loire. These and other saintly folk were setting the stage for the diversity of the French wine industry of today.

Then came Charlemagne. In a crucial battle at Poitiers in A.D. 732, the Frankish leader, Charles Martel (sinisterly known as "the Hammer"), had stopped in its tracks the northward advance of the forces of Islam out of Italy and France. His son, Pepin the Short, established a determinedly Christian kingdom at Aachen in Germany. In turn, Pepin's son, Charles—our Charlemagne-to-be—extended the Frankish Empire in all directions. All powerful now, he was crowned by the Pope as emperor of the Holy Roman Empire in A.D. 800 (Plate 62).

With so much political strife at last resolved, the early 9th century A.D. was a time of renewed prosperity for Europe. Whereas the Rhine had been a difficult-to-control frontier for the Romans, it now became the heart of economic activity in Charlemagne's lands. He granted lands to nobles, bishops, and monasteries, and gave rights to settlements to hold markets and fairs that soon would attract merchants from much further afield. Charlemagne's personal fascination with viticulture meant that he encouraged every attempt be made to plant thousands of acres of new vineyards around the dozens of new abbeys and fast-growing towns of northern Europe.

There was a snag associated with the speed at which this economic expansion occurred. As we know, Roman agriculturists, such as Columella and Varro, had pointed out long ago that viticulture demanded, among other things, an appreciable capital investment and a skilled but low-cost work force (see Plate 18). To this end, during the Republican era, the Romans had turned their slave system to good account. In 9th century A.D. Europe, however, there were no slaves, and there was a shortage of peasantry that could be called upon to transform what were then just huge land tracts of wilderness forest and marshland into easily plowed fields. Church authorities negotiated a partnership with free laborers that worked out well enough. It amounted to a profit-sharing arrangement based on the laborers' sweat equity; it persists today as a system known as *metayage*. Meanwhile, however, a number of monastic orders—particularly the Benedictines—flung themselves whole-heartedly into the process of land recovery. For the monks, the turning of the soil and its transformation to rich fertility was a labor of love, and the intensity with which they worked lifted the scale of European

wine-production to a new level.

Over the subsequent centuries, the will-power of bishops and priors often clashed with that of kings and courtiers, as the profits of wine production swelled the Church's coffers year-in and year-out. Most times, the Church leaders carried the day. Meanwhile the monastic orders squabbled amongst themselves over the perceived merits or evils of drink, and thus the appropriateness of their involvement in its production. On the one side there was a paternal tolerance akin to that displayed by early Christian leaders over the matter of pagan-style wine offerings at the graves of saints (see XVI: Religious Overtones):

> . . .making allowance for the weakness of the infirm, we think a *hermina* [half a pint] of wine a day is sufficient for each one. But to whom God has granted the endurance of abstinence, let them know that they will have their special reward. (*The Rule of St. Benedict* XL)

On the other side was the likes of the Irish missionary, St. Columbanus, who founded monasteries in Alsace and insisted on his followers living a relentlessly austere life that certainly was not to be tainted by something as morale-softening as wine.[61] All the time, however, the sheer wealth of the Church overall underpinned ongoing investment in the technology of viticulture that was to ensure French and German wines their eventual high stature in the world marketplace.[62, 63]

At this point, to properly round out my story, I must turn back the clock a while. We have seen that the fall of the Western Empire could be characterized as the result of wars among squabbling factions. In the Eastern Empire, the Roman demise was quite different—on a grand scale, swift and bloody. By A.D. 638, the forces of Islam had overwhelmed the entire Eastern Mediterranean shoreline. If you were a vintner in that landscape, in Syria or Judaea, you would have known well enough what to expect from this change of political order. The prophet Mohammed had already been dead six years by then. During the last decade of his life, however, the non-Roman Middle East had undergone a most remarkable switch in attitude towards

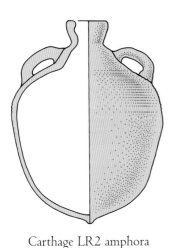

Carthage LR2 amphora

PLATE 63:

This amphora appears in quantity at the port of Carthage in north Africa—hence its type designation—but it has a widespread distribution, particularly around the Aegean and along the west coast of the Black Sea. It may have been made somewhere close to Athens (Peacock and Williams 1986). Its form persisted from the 4th to the early 7th century A.D., at which point its production abruptly ceased. Its demise most likely is connected to the disruption of sea trade that resulted from Islamic incursions along the coastline of Asia Minor and into the Aegean (see Chadwick and Evans 1989).

wine. Here were several cultures that had enjoyed wine for millennia past, yet a single verse in the Koran—"Satan seeks to stir up emnity and hatred among you by means of wine and gambling. . .Will you not abstain from them?" (*The Table* V.90)—had led to a ban on wine that took effect almost overnight.[64]

Wine exportation from Palestine to the West had been booming during the previous century and a half (see Plate 11); now it was reduced to nothing. As the core of Byzantine Empire shrank back into Asia Minor and Greece, the eastern sea-lanes of the Mediterranean fell under Islamic control as well, cutting off Byzantine trade to north Africa, including that with the once powerful port of Carthage (Plate 63). The clergy of Gaul no longer could savor the fine white wines of Gaza.

There was cautious rebellion against such a ban on many fronts, and not a little ambiguity about its practicalities. Mohammed himself drank a date wine called *nabidh*, yet flogged those who violated his injunction against wine from the grape. His favorite wife, Ayesha, argued that what the Prophet *really* had meant was that you could drink but must not get drunk. Mohammed's successor, Caliph Umar ibn Al-Khattab, took a hard line on the matter, trying to pre-empt any risk of drunkenness becoming widespread among his subjects by using the whip ever more viciously on those who imbibed at all. In later

times, however, courtiers and poets—most notably, the Persian Omar Khayyam in the 11th century A.D.—all but ignored the ban and interwove the notions of physical love, mortality, and the pleasures of wine in ways that recalled the subtler phrases of Ovid and Horace, centuries before.

The pendulum of tolerance swung back and forth. In the mid 9th century A.D., the Caliph Mutawakkil threw wine parties that recalled the Greek *symposium* or the Roman *commisatio*—a meal first, then a rigmarole of dressing up in finery well-laced with perfumes before settling down to some really heavy drinking. The different wines would be served in a prescribed order, and the guests would include a connoisseur or two who would wax lyrical about the bouquet of each one.[65] In contrast, several 10th century A.D. caliphs took measures to prevent wine production. These measures included both practical acts such as throwing thousands of jars of honey into the Nile and ripping up vineyards, and the simple bureaucratic procedure of raising taxes on wine merchants. In contrast again, if a miniature by the Sultan Muhammed is to be taken at its face value, early in the 16th century A.D. not only were the party guests plied heavily with wine, but it was even served on high to the angels themselves.

Moral purges came and went, but there was an ongoing tolerance in the Islamic World for wine as

والاول وتم ومنفعت كلام البسا نا با

Grape vine (*vitis sylvestris*)

PLATE 64:

Though Islamic illuminators remained faithful to the medical principles expressed in Dioscorides' *De Materia Medica*, their depiction of the plantstuffs tended to be much more elaborate. This early 13th century A.D. Syrian illustration is typical (cf. the 5th century A.D. folios in Plates 45, 53, 56 and 75). As early as the 9th century A.D., some Byzantine illuminators of Dioscorides' manuscripts were adding human figures alongside the medicinal herbs, so that they could point to the afflication against which a particular plant's extract was effective. Islamic artists followed suit with such "explanatory images" towards the end of the 11th century A.D.

a medicinal. By the 9th century A.D., the libraries of Jundi-Shapur just outside Baghdad were becoming crowded with Classical treatises on all manner of scientific topics, and Islamic scholars were devoting their whole lives to their translation and interpretation. The Islamic fascination with medical works was intense, with the son of a druggist, Huynan ibn Ishaq al-'Abadi (died, A.D. 873) gaining particular recognition for his translation of the late 2nd century A.D. treatises of Galen of Pergamum. Huynan's nephew, Hubaysh ibn al-Hassan carried on the family tradition with distinction, translating the late 5th century B.C. treatises of Hippocrates of Cos, and the mid 1st century A.D. *De Materia Medica* of Dioscorides (Plate 64). Their views on wine tend to mirror their Classical antecedents, of course, as do those of several of the later Islamic physicians. For example, there are echoes of a convivium guests' exchange of opinion in Plutarch's *Table Talk*, in the observation:

> To give wine to youths is like adding fire to a fire already prepared with matchwood. Young adults should take it in moderation. But elderly persons may take as much as

they can tolerate. Wine is borne better in a cold country than in a hot one. (Ibn Sina of Afshena [known as Avicenna], *Canon* 810)

When those words were written in the early 11th century A.D., the Islamic mood was for tolerance; scholarship was thriving, and innovative thought was everywhere and encouraged.

Then came the Ottamans. The Ottoman state originated in Asia Minor at the turn of the 14th century A.D. as a force bent on crusading against the neighboring Christian lands. In A.D. 1453 the Sultan Mehmet II took Constantinople, and by A.D. 1516 the Ottoman army held the entire Eastern Mediterranean coastline and was heading for Belgrade. Vineyards that had persevered through the past brief eras of Islamic moral anguish over wine, now were truly devastated, as villages were destroyed and essential irrigation systems were ruined. Jewish and Christian traders, who to a large extent controlled the infrastructure of the Eastern wine trade, fled to the safer confines of the Byzantine world. Many of the ancient wine-growing regions in the Near East have never recovered, even to this day.[66]

So it is that our own era sits at the end of a long and winding path of change in the story of wine. Viticulture is now well-established in America, but it was not always so. During the latter half of the 16th century, the Europeans who settled at various points along the eastern seaboard were quick to harvest native wild grapes and convert them into wine. The modest success of those endeavors encouraged the importation of the domesticated European vine (*Vitis vinifera*), along with skilled vine-dressers, with the intent of mimicking the lifestyle of their homelands, be it England or France. But very few of the transplanted vines survived. Extremely cold winters simply killed many of them outright, and high humidity during the growing season encouraged the spread of crop-ruining mildew and other diseases. If that wasn't bad enough, in several areas, *Vitis vinifera* was decimated by something it had never experienced before—the native root-louse, *phylloxera*. During the late 18th century, domestication of several native American species of vine—particularly *Vitis labrusca*—was quite successful, but the wines struggled in the marketplace because of what was referred to as a "foxy" flavor.

At much the same time, a variety of *Vitis vinifera* was introduced on the Western American seaboard, thriving well there as the so-called "mission grape." Even then, the early Californian wine-growers struggled to gain any consistency among their products. Initially, the means of storage they had at their disposal—sewn-up hides and earthenware jugs—simply was inadequate, and spoilage percentages were distressingly high; and even when the use of wooden casks became prevalent, too much wine still went sour.

What were they doing wrong, these pioneer vintners?—one after another of them pondered the problem. Improvement came quickly when it was realized that careless picking allowed too many moldy or rotten grapes to slip into the pulp. Output improved again when the American vintners followed the lead of their French contemporaries and fumigated their casks with burning sulfur before re-use (see Endnote 63).

The learning curve for the American wine industry was painfully slow in its upturn.[67] But universal recognition that good hygiene was the key to high profits meant that during the 1950s the American wine industry—particularly the sector in California—was flourishing nationally, and was on the verge of entering the world stage. Thirty years on from there, the output of American vineyards had tripled to 332 million U.S. gallons per year; today, two decades later, it has almost doubled again. We can expect yet a further growth over the next two decades, possibly one just as dramatic. For it is clear that the American palate is shifting to wine more and more. In the 1950s importation of wine ran to around 5.8 million U.S. gallons; three decades later, that figure also had risen even faster than domestic output, to a staggering 72.7 million U.S. gallons.

What of Italy, where my story began?—so much has changed. As of 1996, Italy ranked a very close second to France, with an annual wine production of 1.55 million U.S. gallons; Spain ranked third, producing just about half as much as Italy, and the United States ranked fourth, with 0.49 million U.S. gallons.[68] The focus of Italian production has shifted northward, however, particularly to the region of Veneto, at the head of the Adriatic. In the southwest corner of that region lies Verona. Its wines gained a good reputation as early as the 6th century A.D., and today that is the area for the finest dry white Soave, red Valpolicella. From there too comes the sweet and red Recioto made from sun-dried grapes, which surely has a Roman match in *passum* (see Plate 32). It is this area that produces close to 20% of the wines most carefully regulated for quality by the Italian government—those with credentials that abide by the rules of the Denominazione de Origine Controllata e Garantitita [DOCG] and the slightly less stringent Denominazione de Origine Controllata [DOC].

In Latium, the home of the emperor Augustus' favorite Setinian, far less wine is produced today. Even though more than 127,000 acres are given over to grape-growing—almost three times that of the Veneto region—only about 6.3% of DOGC and DOC quality wines are produced there. In Campania, the home of Rome's beloved Falernian, the level of wine production is lower still, though innovative attempts to re-create authentic Pompeian vintages do keep alive the mystique of that region (Plate 65). Meanwhile, the region of Apulia, home of the Aminaean grape that was the staple of the Roman wine industry, continues in a similar role today, some 0.36 million acres—about 19% of the Italian peninsula's vineyards—producing wine for Italy's mass market.

As I look back over the past few thousand years, it seems to me that wine has always been a source of some small pleasure at all levels of society. The middle classes of Rome might not have drunk Falernian, but there were many medium quality wines that would complement their modest evening meals. We can be sure they knew where to find them, just as many of us have learned to be bargain-hunters for a tasty *vin ordinaire*, as well. Thankfully, we are spared the experience of Rome's slave society, their ration of wine usually being the product of waste grapes rather than something from a named vineyard. Nonetheless, we must want to believe that even some of this *lora*, of an evening, helped to ease the pain of those no-rights people, young and old alike, and carried them into dreams of kinder, gentler worlds far removed from their everyday experience. Wine in Roman times was what some people think it is today: a salve for the body *and* the soul.

PLATE 65:

This pergola-style vineyard has been staked out at the *House of Eusino* in Pompeii by the Mastroberadino Winery of Avellino. The planting pattern drew its inspiration from vine-root remains and stake cavities found during the excavation of the ancient cattle market (*Foro Boario*) to the north of Pompeii's amphitheater (Jashemski 1973).
The Mastroberadinos specialize in making wine from ancient grape varietals, including the Greco and Aglianico that were introduced on the Italian peninsula by the Greeks some 2,500 years ago, the sugar-rich Fiano that thrives on the Irpinia Hills northeast of Avellino, and the Coda di Volpe that thrives on the black volcanic soils on the lower slopes of Mt. Vesuvius. The latter two varietals are indigenous to Italy; both are mentioned by Pliny in his detailed description of vine- and grape-types which flourished in his day.

The *Vitis apiana* is so called because bees are specially fond of it. It has two varieties which also are covered with down in the young state. . .The vines do not object to cold situations; nevertheless no others rot more quickly from rain. (Pliny, *Natural History* XIV.25, for Fiano)

On the other hand the ashy grape and the dusky grape and the donkey-grape are condemned even by their appearance, though this is less the case with the *alopecis*, which resembles a fox's brush. (Pliny, *Natural History* XIV.25, for Coda di Volpe)

A CLOSING THOUGHT ON BOTH WINE AND HUMAN MORALITY....

Some say that in this city of Lyon there were two people, a man and a wife, who were distinguished members of a senatorial family. Since they had no children when they were about to die, they left the cathedral as their heir. The man died first and was buried in the church of St. Mary. For an entire year his wife visited this church; she diligently prayed, attended the celebrations of Mass every day, and made offerings on behalf of the memory of her husband. Beause she never doubted that through the mercy of the Lord her deceased husband would repose in Paradise on the day that she made an offering to the Lord on behalf of his soul, she always presented a pint of wine from Gaza to the sanctuary of the holy church. But the subdeacon was a sinful man and kept the wine from Gaza for his own drinking pleasure. Since the woman never came forward for the grace of communicating during the celebration of the Eucharist, he instead offered very bitter vinegar in the chalice.

When God was pleased to expose this fraud, the husband appeared to his wife in a vision and said: 'Alas, alas, my most beloved wife. How did the effort of my life in this world reach such a point that I now taste vinegar in my offering?' The woman replied to him: 'In truth, I have not forgotten your charity and I have always offered the most fragrant wine from Gaza in the sanctuary of my God on behalf of your repose.' She awoke, thought about the vision, and did not forget it. As was her custom, she got up for matins. After matins were over and Mass had been celebrated, she approached the cup of salvation. When she sipped the chalice, the vinegar was so bitter that she thought her teeth would have fallen out if she had not swallowed the drink quickly. Then she rebuked the subdeacon, and what had been done sinfully and fraudulently was corrected. But I think that this miracle did not happen without the merit of the good deed performed by the woman. (Gregory of Tours, *Glory of the Confessors*.LXIV)

Massive silver dish from the Mildenhall Treasure, decorated with all manner of scenes of Bacchic revelry 4th century A.D.

Bacchus I saw on distant crags—believe me, you of after time—teaching hymns, and I beheld the nymphs his pupils, and the goat-footed satyrs with their pointed ears. . .Meet, too, it is to sing of the crown of your consort deified, set now among the stars, and Pentheus' palace overthrown in dire destruction, and the fatal end of the Thracian Lycurgus. (Horace, *Odes* II.xix)

Black hellebore (*Helleborus niger*) from Discorides' *De Materia Medica*

If you wish to make a laxative wine, after vintage, when the vines are trenched, expose the roots of as many vines as you think you will need for the purpose and mark them; isolate and clear roots. Pound roots of black hellebore in the mortar and apply around vines. Cover the roots with old manure, old ashes, and two parts of earth, and cover the whole with earth.

(Cato, *On Agriculture* VII.82)

XVIII

ENDNOTES

I   This is how Odysseus spoke of Maronean wine, as he and his companions prepared to meet the monstrous Cyclops:

> This man [Maron, son of Euanthes] made me some fine presents: he gave me seven talents of wrought gold, with a mixing bowl of silver, and he drew off for me as well a full dozen jars of mellow unmixed wine. And a wonderful drink it was. It had been kept secret from all his serving-men and maids, in fact from everyone in the house but himself, his good wife, and a single stewardess. When they drank this red and honeyed vintage, he used to pour one cupful of wine into twenty of water, and the sweet fumes that came up from the bowl were irresistible—those were occasions when abstinence could have no charms. (Homer's *The Odyssey* IX.197)

Clearly, this wine was extremely strong: something closer to a one-to-three dilution of wine was considered more appropriate at the Roman dinner table (see XI: A Matter of Etiquette).

2   Quality Roman wines rarely were laid away for more than twenty years, but the much longer kept Opimian vintages, even if they became over-ripe, were always acceptable as a seasoning for lesser, younger wines. Opimian vintages also were regarded as an excellent fiscal investment; Pliny (*Natural History* XIV.53) rated it as more worthwhile than legal money-lending.

3   The following quotation, which dates to the early 1st century A.D., provides a window onto the nature of this trade at the coastal ports of southern Gaul:

And many of these trees, even in the variegation of the grain, are not inferior to the thyine [citrus-tree] wood for the purposes of table-making. These, the people bring down to the emporium of Genua, as well as flocks, hides and honey, and receive therefore a return cargo of olive oil and Italian wine. (Strabo, *Geography* IV.6)

4 Two Classical writers, Plutarch and Livy—in *Roman History* V.xxxiii and *Lives: Camillus.*xv, respectively—actually attribute the Celts' invasions of northern Italy at various times from the early 4th century B.C. onwards to their passion for Italian wine. There is evidence for viticulture in southern Gaul as early as the mid 2nd century B.C., though this was an agricultural venture which, along with olive-growing, the Romans tried to prohibit to protect Italian trade profits (see Goudineau [1983], referring to the text of Cicero, *On The Republic* III.9).

5 Current thinking is that the European species of the vine (*Vitis sylvestris*) originated along the mild and wet southern coastline of the Black Sea where it still climbs wild in the forest canopy. Out of this viticultural heartland, the vine migrated westward, gradually by nature to some extent, but more aggressively whenever immigrants took plant cuttings with them. It was introduced into Italy by Greek farmers who settled in several regions along the coastline from just north of Naples to the peninsula's "heel" at Tarentum (see Plate IB). The vines that Mediterranean peoples took with them into temperate Europe were not hardy, but they survived long enough to cross-pollinate with the indigenous wild varieties. Out of the resulting jumble came wild seedlings which combined many of the good qualities of each parent: self-pollinating plants that had hybrid vigor and could provide a range of new wine aromas and flavors. The wild ("savage") component of this hybridization is reflected in the names of many of France's most popular grapes such as the Sauvignon (Wagner 1974).

6 During the period of about 10 B.C.–A.D. 60, a few audacious businessmen applied a quirky variant to the usual pattern of movement of wine from northern Spain. Though much of the wine was carried in the standard amphorae of the day (Plate 66), a lot of it also was put in *dolia* (i.e., massive vessels with a capacity of close to 40 amphorae: see XIX: Units of Capacity) that were a fixture of the ship (Aubert 1994). A stamp impression C[aius] PIRANVS indicates that these dolia were manufactured exclusively(?) by one family business, the Pirani of Minturnae. The gain in the wine-weight to container-weight ratio that the dolium offered over the amphora was appreciable, perhaps as high as 70%. The offloading procedure of dolia-to-dolia at a port such as Ostia, which could handle such a procedure, must have been quite efficient. What was sacrificed, however, was the cargo stability that went with the traditional layering of amphorae which interlocked each group of bases with the underlying array of necks and handles. The fact that at least seven dolia-rigged ships sank en route to Italy may explain why this system of transport eventually was abandoned.

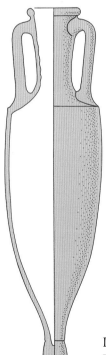

PLATE 66:

Dressel 2 amphora (after Peacock and Williams [1989])

7 During the mid 2nd century A.D., at the height of its prosperity under the patronage of the emperors Hadrian and Antoninus Pius, Carthage also probably had a population approaching half a million. Three cities in Asia Minor—Antioch, Pergamum, and

Ephesus—whose fortunes were revived at that time, probably were home to more than 100,000 inhabitants each (Harris 1993).

8 The clearest archaeological evidence for this agricultural decline on the Italian mainland comes from a villa preserved at Settefinestre, situated about 90 miles northwest of Rome close to the coastal colony of Cosa (Potter 1987; Aubert 1994). Its estate probably covered just over 300 U.S. acres, about 40% of which was committed to vineyards that are thought in its late Republican heyday, to have been producing more than 29,000 U.S. gallons of wine a year (see also Endnote 21). By about A.D. 160, however, the Settefinestre villa was crumbling into ruins. There is also some literary evidence for the widespread abandonment and destruction of estates in Campania during the Antonine period (Carandini and Panella 1981), the potential for economic recovery surely being stymied by the persistence of the plague that struck Rome in A.D. 167 (Fleming 1999).

The mechanisms by which wine was being traded between estates and cities within Italy are somewhat hidden from us today by the gradual shift away from pottery amphorae to perishable containers such as wooden casks and leather skins. But the mid 5th century A.D., administrative documents indicate that in A.D. 395 there were more than 300,000 acres of abandoned land (*agri deserti*) in Campania alone—almost a tenth of the total farmland of that region.

9 The ups-and-downs of Gaul's economic fortunes are discussed in Galliou (1981), and a similar discussion of the fluctuating fortunes of the cities at the frontiers on the Rhine and the Danube is provided by King (1990). For a valuable review of the impact of the various events, political and natural, that so influenced the economy of the Roman World overall during the 3rd and 4th centuries A.D., see MacMullen (1988).

10 The basic structure of a wine press in early Judaea was a treading floor, a filtering basin, and a collection vat—sometimes two or three of them—all parts being cut into hard limestone rock wherever it was exposed (Ahlström 1978; Dar 1999). These presses are notoriously difficult to date since they would

have been kept trash-free and clean from year-to-year of usage. More elaborate presses that had vats floored with a water-tight mosaic or well-matched paving stones and surrounding structures built of precisely laid ashlar stonework, most likely date to the early Byzantine era (Mayerson 1985; Roll and Ayalon 1981: see also Plate 28 here).

11 Early pilgrims ventured into lonely desert areas in search of scriptural history in the Palestinian landscape, and so pioneered the paths to holy places. Around A.D. 383, during her journey towards Jerusalem, the lady Egeria sent this message to her friends back in Gaul (see Chadwick and Evans [1989]): "It may help you, loving sisters, the better to picture what happened in these places when you read the holy books of Moses."

The 5th century A.D. priest, Cyril of Scythopolis, provides glowing accounts of the houses set up by monks in the Judaean desert where any pilgrim could rest and eat. Meanwhile, in and around Jersualem, there were all manner of places to stay (Wilkinson 1977). Those who came from the emperor's court most likely would head for the house established on the Mount of Olives by Melania the Elder and Rufinus of Aquileia sometime after A.D. 380—a somewhat too comfortable place for true pilgrims, in the opinion of Jerome of Stridon who founded a rather more austere place of rest close to the Church of the Nativity in Bethlehem (Hunt 1982).

12 Thus far, only nine wine presses have been excavated in the Negev, to the south and east of the port of Gaza and the city of Elusa (see Plate 12), but their vats range in capacity from about 590 to 2,000 U.S. gallons (Mayerson 1985). With the entire process—grape treading, must fermentation, and collection of the new wine—usually taking about seven days, and a harvesting period of six weeks or more, we are talking here of an annual production running as high as 55,000 U.S. gallons—wine enough to satisfy the needs of both the local townsfolk and the streams of transitory pilgrims, with ample to spare for export to the West.

13 Thus, in A.D. 584 during a seemingly amiable exchange between the Frankish monk Claudius

and king Chilperic's ex-treasurer, Eberulf:

> . . .'I should delight to drain a cup at thy lodging, if the wine was mixed with spice, or if thy mightiness would ask for a draught of stronger wine for me.' Eberulf was overjoyed at these words, and answered that he had what was desired. . .And he sent his servants, one after the other to get stronger wines, those of Latium and those of Gaza. (Gregory of Tours, *History of the Franks* VII.29)

While those servants were out of the way, however, Claudius tried to murder Eberulf, only to be speared to death himself just minutes later by the latter's followers—such was the outcome of these Christian pleasantries.

14   The influence sometimes wielded by educated slaves in the business affairs of their master is well illustrated by Trimalchio's observation: "Then, as the gods willed, I became the real master of the house, and simply had his brains in my pocket." (Petronius, *Satyricon.* 76). We can assume that at some point Trimalchio served as an estate bailiff (*vilicus*) with managerial responsibilities ranging from keeping track of the yields and sale of all products to buying equipment, slaves, fodder, and so on. He also dealt with securities and credit as well, even though the early Roman agronomists urged landowners to keep this type of activity under personal control (*sic* Trimalchio's activities) (see Aubert [1994], citing Cato, *On Agriculture* II.1-7).

Of course, Trimalchio was a fictitious character. But he could well have been modeled after someone like the slave Clarus. During the middle years of the 1st century A.D. he was responsible for at least the production of amphorae on behalf of Gaius Laecanius Bassus who owned a sizable estate at Fasana, southeast of Tergeste (modern Trieste) (Aubert 1994). Various texts and the stamp impression C LAEC[anii] BAS[si]/CLARUS clearly identifies his role as *vilicus*, not just in the manufacture of amphorae, but also of other revenue-raising items such as bricks, tiles, pipes, and lamps.

15   Politicking was everywhere in the manipulation of the business activities surrounding the Roman staples of grain, wine,

and olive oil.

> Once, upon the occasion of a plentiful wine crop, attended with a scarcity of grain, thinking that the fields were neglected through too much attention to the vineyards, he [emperor Domitian] made an edict forbidding anyone to plant more vines in Italy, and ordering that the vineyards in the provinces be cut down, or but half of them at most be left standing; but he did not persist in carrying out this measure. (Suetonius, *Lives of the Caesars* VIII: Domitian. vii) (Plate68)

PLATE 67:

Gold coin (aureus) depicting the emperor Domitian (reigned, A.D. 81-96)

> . . .he became an object of terror and hatred to all, but he was overthrown at last by a conspiracy of his friends and favorite freedmen, to which his wife was also privy. (Suetonius, *Lives of the Caesars* VIII: Domitian.xiv)

In A.D. 90, when the edict was issued, Asia Minor certainly was in the grips of a famine crisis, so the purpose of it appears to have been to increase grain production throughout the Empire (Levick 1982). But it is thought to have had two ulterior motives as well; first of simply reducing pressure on vine-growers on the Italian peninsula, and second of denying the availability of wine in Asia Minor where it might enflame some revolutionary minds among the starving (see Philostratus, *Lives of the Sophists* 520).

The edict might have gone through, but for a surprisingly personal poem that circulated like wildfire through the city immediately after it was proclaimed.

Gnaw at my root as you will; even then shall
I have juice in plenty
To pour upon thee, O goat [Domitian],
when at the altar you stand.
(Suetonius, *Lives of the Caesars* VIII:
Domitian. xiv)

16 Ancient texts also use the term *mucor* ("mold")
to describe wine's deterioration. Though
molds do not grow on wine, a taste of that
kind can result if moldy grapes or unclean
cooperage are used. In general terms though,
mucor probably could be read as an unpleasant
"staleness" or "flatness," whatever the cause
(Amerine 1981; Frier 1983).
One of the reasons that Roman vintners may
have favored allowing the grapes to ripen so
long on the vine was to raise the sugar content
as high as possible. Subsequent fermentation
would yield a wine with a higher alcohol
content that would discourage it from
perishing.
The tactic used so extensively for wine
preservation today—adulteration with
sulphur—apparently was tried in the mid 2nd
century A.D. by the father of the famous
physician, Galen of Pergamum (Nutton
1969). We know now that the presence of
sulfur inhibits the growth of wild yeasts on the
grape skins and reduces oxidation, something
which is particularly important for
maintaining the quality of white wines
(Amerine 1964). Its usage in Roman
viticulture surely would have been extremely
valuable. Yet I am not aware that the idea ever
caught on.

17 There can be little doubt that Columella's
ideas stemmed from the empirical experiences
of many earlier Roman agriculturalists.

To remove a bad odor from wine, heat a
thick clean piece of roofing-tile thoroughly
in the fire. When it is hot coat it with pitch,
attach a string, lower it gently to the bottom
of the jar, and leave the jar sealed for two
days. If the bad odor is removed the first
time, that will be the best; if not, repeat
until the bad odor is removed. (Cato, *On
Agriculture* CX)

But Cato also prescribed to the scientifically
dubious good scent versus bad smell approach
to preservation, taking the same pitch-covered
roofing-tile and spreading on it ". . .aromatic

herbs, rush and the palm which perfumers
keep. . . ." (*On Agriculture* CXIII), before
putting the tile in the amphora and sealing
everything up for a while.

18 Pliny also discussed wine preservatives at some
length and leaned heavily towards the use of
tree resins for that purpose. Chips of sweet-
smelling wood, such as laurel, juniper, mastic,
and terebinth, were added to the must before it
was boiled. Pliny, like Columella, also was
assertive about the need to ensure the
cleanliness of amphorae before their first
filling or their re-use.

Immediately after the rising of the Dog-
Star they should be coated with pitch, and
afterwards washed with sea-water or water
with salt in it, and then sprinkled with
brushwood or else with potter's earth, and
then sprinkled with myrrh, as should be
done with the wine cellars also. (Pliny,
Natural History XIV.112)

The choice of myrrh here seems remarkable,
given that it had to be imported from the
Arabian Peninsula and so was very expensive.
But Pliny was fully aware of the popularity of
myrrh-flavored wine, particularly among
wealthy Romans who identified themselves
with the good taste of Greeks and knew of
several ancient literary allusions to its quality:

But if he has to bring out a sweet wine from
that same cellar, has he got one? Got
one?—myrrh-wine and raisin wine, and
boiled-down must and honey. (Lucius
Aelius, *Pseudolus* 740)

The Romans also often salvaged wine that was
on the point of turning to vinegar by making
it re-ferment on the dried and baked lees of
good wine (see Columella, *On Agriculture*
XII.xxx). Only in the past century has this
tactic been recognized as an effective one
(Majno 1975).

19 Roman lawyers really agonized over what
exactly wine was (Watson 1985). In the
section of the *Digest of Justinian* dealing with
many of the material aspects of legacies,
vinegar was separated out, as one might expect,
but so was spiced wine and concentrated must
". . .because it is prepared rather for preserving
fruit." (Book XXXIII.6). Wine made with the
end-of-season raisins and must flavored with
honey and salt were both legally classified as

wines. But fruit wines prepared from other plantstuffs such as quinces, and mead made of fermented honey and water were not. If the provisions of the will indicated a bequest of so many amphorae of wine, should that be read just as a measure of the amount of wine, or were the containers themselves necessarily part of the legacy?—apparently so; but not so for wooden casks since they were just the storage unit in the cellar while the wine was maturing. Wrangling over such matters might seem petty to most of us today. But the inheritance of a fine wine cellar was just as valued in the Roman world as it is today. For example, the orator, Quintus Hortensius Hortalus—best known for his rivalry with Cicero during some of the latter's famous trials—left over ten thousand jars of Chian wine to his next-of-kin when he died in 49 B.C. (see Pliny, *Natural History* XIV.96).

20   Of course, like any business venture dependent upon the vagaries of the weather, vineyards and those who marketed their products could fall on hard times. A case in point is described in an Egyptian papyrus document of A.D. 330 known as the *Meletian Schism*. This text acknowledges the sufferings of a certain wine-dealer, Pamonthius, who was so deeply in debt that he was forced to sell not only all of his property and his wardrobe but also to hand over his children to his creditors. Though it was illegal to pledge one's children as a security—and so, in the eventuality of default, commit them to slavery—such a practice was quite widespread (Bell 1924).

21   Supplementary information about the profitability of early Italian vineyards comes from the excavation and interpretation of the estate of Settefinestre which lies in the Valle d'Oro about two miles from the ancient port of Cosa (near modern Orbetello). To support the staff of the estate's villa, it is believed that the farming was mixed—about 200 *iugera* given over to a vineyard, 30 *iugera* to woodland, and 270 *iugera* to agricultural land and pasture (Carandini 1980). Small clusters of rooms (*cellae*), identified as slave quarters, suggest a slave population of about 40; roughly three-quarters of them were involved in cultivation of the vineyard and of wine production at the three torcular wine-presses found in the villa.

The yield of this estate's vineyard has been estimated at 215 *cullei* of wine which, in export, might be valued at about 64,000 *sestertii*. Those figures suggest a profit of around 1,500 *sestertii* per slave (Aubert 1994). That might not seem too significant an income. But clusters of secondary buildings around the Settefinestre and other estates dotted throughout the Valle d'Oro seem to have been properties of land-holders who could provide supplementary manpower on an as-needed basis, most obviously at harvest times; late summer for grapes and grain, winter for olives. A timely mix of slave- and hired-labor could increase the estate's profitability by a factor of two (Rathbone 1981).

22   Of course, all around thriftiness always added to the profitability of any ancient vineyard.

> When the weather is bad and no other work can be done, clear out manure for the compost heap; clean thoroughly the ox stalls, sheep pens, barnyard and farmstead; and mend dolia with lead, or hoop them with thoroughly dried oak wood. If you mend it carefully, or hoop it tightly, closing the cracks with cement and pitching it thoroughly, you can make any jar serve as a wine jar (*dolium vinarium*). (Cato, *On Agriculture* XXXIX).

23   Cicero lived through the turmoils of the mid 1st century B.C. power struggle within the ruling triumvirate of Crassus, Pompey, and Caesar from which the last eventually was to emerge as dictator of the Republic. Cicero's eloquent pleadings at the trials of several leading political figures—among them Publius Sestius and Marcus Fonteius (see Plate 16)—who found themselves caught up in this struggle provide a wealth of information about how such people conducted their fiscal affairs. After he freed him, Cicero's use of the term *amicus* to describe the bond between himself and his Greek-born secretary Tiro indicates well enough how the Latin vocabulary of friendship could glide over differences in social status when it came to business relationships (see *Letters to Friends* XVI.16). But there were real risks in doing things this way (D'Arms 1981). One trader, Licinius Nepos, who had hoped to become rich through such wheeling-and-dealing, complained in his epitaph that

".. .he was deceived by hope, and by many friends." (ILS 7513) And, as Trimalchio put it: "You know how it is.. .the moment business takes a bad turn your friends [*amici*] desert you." (Petronius, *Satyricon*. 38)

Among the Roman patricians who owned so much of the Italian farmland, trust was a key factor in business dealings, to the point where for some it was morally proper to take a loss on a contract rather than upset established relationships.

> Other people visit their estates to come away richer than before, but I go only to return the poorer. I had sold my grape harvest to the dealers [*negotiatores*], who were eager to buy, when the price quoted at the time was tempting and prospects seemed good. Their hopes were frustrated. It would have been simplest to give them all the same rebate, but hardly fair; and I hold the view that one of the most important things is to practice justice in private as well as public life, in small matters as in great, and apply it to one's own affairs no less than to other people's. For, if we say with the Stoics that 'all offences are equal', the same applies to merits. Accordingly, I returned to everyone an eighth of the sum he had spent so that 'none should depart without a gift of mine'. Then I made a special provision for those who had invested very large sums in their purchase, since they had been the greater service to me and theirs was the greater loss. I therefore allowed everyone whose purchases had cost him more than 10,000 sesterces a tenth of everything he had spent above that sum, in addition to the original eighth which was a sort of general grant. (Pliny the Younger, *Letters* VIII.ii, to Calvisius Rufus)

The rather complex calculations underlying this negotiation are described in the subsequent paragraph, along with some bonuses for those who had paid in advance.

Even when the grain and vines crops were reasonably plentiful, though, it seems that prices sometimes were forced artificially low, making it difficult for a small farmer to survive.

> An amphora of wine goes for twenty asses, a modius of wheat for four. Drunk and

dyspeptic, the farmer has nothing. (Martial, *Epigrams* XII.76)

24 With the vast network of new colonies that were created during the Republican period, the proper allocation of land to the settlers was a serious matter (Potter 1990). The process spawned a major civil service department within Roman State government that, at the beginning of the 2nd century B.C., was handling claims for at least a million *iugera* [0.62 million U.S. acres] for a hundred thousand families. The plots themselves were awarded by lottery. Whether the land was to be divided into squares (*limitatio*)—the process that we call "centuriation"—or into strips, rectangular or irregular (*strigae* and *subseciva*, respectively), all of the boundaries had to be defined and marked with care.

Even before then, however, the needs of colonization had wrought some huge changes in the Italian landscape. For example, in the region of Apulia on the northern side of a colony founded in 314 B.C. at Luceria (modern Lucera), close to 10,000 *iugera* of land was parceled off into about fifty plots under this scheme. In the vicinity of nearby Foggia, centuriation was applied to an area eight times that size.

In terms of the story of Roman viticulture, perhaps the most important program of centuriation occurred in the floodplain of the Po valley. It was drained and brought under control by Roman engineers to allow the cultivation of vast amounts of wheat and turnip cabbage (*rapum*) (see Strabo, *Geography* V.I), and of millet, which was primarily a fodder crop though it could be used to make a flavored wine as well (see Pliny, *Natural History* XIV.101). Viticulture flourished on the Po Plain. It had excellent economic viability because of the Via Aemilia that was built by the consul Marcus Aemilius Lepidus in 187 B.C. to link various colonia dotted along the northeastern side of the Appenines between the Adriatic port of Ariminum and Placentia (modern Rimini and Piacenza, respectively).

25 I have already noted the Celtic preference for wooden casks for their storage of wine (see II: Markets Old and New); and I have discussed the adverse impact on wine production that must have occurred as the successive waves of

Germanic tribes surged across the Gallic landscape from the mid 3rd century A.D. onwards (see Section IV: A Broader Picture). So we can assume that cask production was difficult during these periods of disruption as well.

Our only other significant source on the use of casks elsewhere in the Empire comes to us amid a lengthy discussion of the history and character of the Emilia-Romagna region of northeastern Italy that flanks the south side of the course of the Po river:

> The country has wonderful pitch works, also; and, as for the wine, the quantity is indicated by the jars, for the wooden ones are larger than houses; and the good supply of the pitch helps much towards the excellent smearing that the jars receive. (Strabo, *Geography* V.2)

At the Adriatic edge of that region lies the port city of Ravenna which became the imperial capital in A.D. 402 just as barbarian hordes were sweeping into northern Italy. There, in A.D. 410, protected on the landward side by marshes and numerous tributaries of the Po, the emperor Honorius was able to wait out and defy Alaraic the Visigoth, even as the latter overwhelmed the rest of the Italian Peninsula. In turn, Ravenna proved to be a safe haven for the barbarian kings of Italy, until it was captured in A.D. 540 by the forces of the emperor Justinian. So we can imagine that Emilia-Romagna wine production was disturbed severely several times during both the 5th and early 6th centuries A.D. and that the supplementary craft of cask-making also suffered during that period.

26   The rapid emergence of the Italian glassworking industry during the first couple of decades of the 1st century A.D. owed much to the popularity of glass wine beakers. The glass at that time tended to have a slightly aqua-blue or light green tinge to it, but its general translucency set it apart from pottery with which it had to compete most strongly in the marketplace (see Plates 26 and 27)—put simply, you could see what you were drinking (Fleming 1999).

Enslaved Hellenistic glassworkers brought with them the skills to produce mold-cast glass wine cups and wine-mixing bowls that truly were some of the most colorful ever produced to this day. Many of the vessels copied those carved from semi-precious hardstones, such as sardonyx and agate, that were then so popular among Rome's wealthy (Plate 68B, detail A). Others mimicked the mosaic patterning of earlier Eastern Mediterranean glassware but with an extra degree of sophistication in the complexity of the multi-colored canes from which they were formed (Plate 68B, details B–D).

Then, in the mid 1st century A.D., there was a sharp and, to a large extent, still ill-explained swing of the pendulum away from brightly colored glassware towards completely colorless wares (Plate 69). The extensive use of faceting in these ware's decoration suggests that the glassworkers were imitating the decoration on elite vessels carved from rock crystal though when these workers would have seen such vessels is uncertain (Vickers 1996). There is some suggestion that glassworkers were provided pattern books for this purpose and for similar copying of metalwares.

27   We can get a sense of how the agricultural activity of Spain might have been affected by Severus's actions by looking at the olive–growing industry there. During its heyday, the olive orchards of the Guadalquivir river valley of Baetica province alone may have comprised more than 12 million trees (Raven 1993). Aside from the massive labor force required to care for and harvest these trees, there had to have been a matching mass production of about 700,000 pottery amphorae, just to provide for the transport overseas of both the olives themselves and the huge amounts of oil squeezed from them (Mattingly 1988). Baetican wine production during the 2nd century A.D. may well have been operating on a comparable scale. Severus, and Caracalla who succeeded him, both imposed an imperial monopoly over what remained of the Spanish wine trade, requiring that amphorae be stamped with various codes that always would include the mark AVG as an abbreviation for the royal title of Augustus.

28   I have followed academic convention here, in labeling the epidemic of circa A.D. 167-180 as the plague. In reality, however, it may have comprised several different infections,

PLATE 68A:

Gold coin (*aureus*) depicting the emperor Augustus (reigned, 27 B.C.–A.D. 14)

> Considering it also of great importance to keep the people pure and unsullied by any taint of foreign or servile blood, he was more chary of conferring Roman citizenship. (Suetonius, *Lives of the Caesars:* Augustus.iii)

Nonetheless, it was the work forces of skilled foreign slaves that ensured the eventual success of the Roman glassworking industry during Augustus' reign.

PLATE 68B:

Mosaic glassware patterns for mold-cast, ribbed glass cups: A: "oxyx-ware," and B–D: multiple cane wares (various color mixtures) (after Fleming [1999])

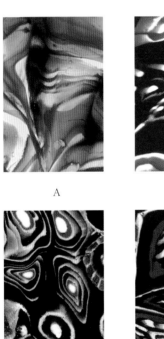

A

B

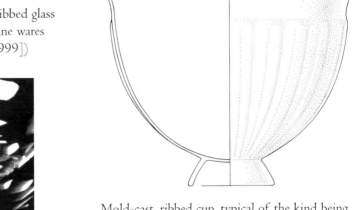

Mold-cast, ribbed cup, typical of the kind being produced in Rome's outskirts during the early 1st century A.D. (Fleming 1999).

C

D

PLATE 69:

Faceted, colorless glass beaker (Ht., 6.7 inches) from Pompeii (after Harden [1987]) Mid 1st century A.D.

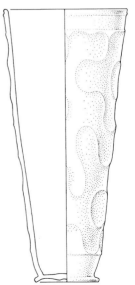

including something akin to modern smallpox (Jackson 1988). Whatever it was precisely, the most respected physician of the day, Galen of Pergamum, played down the significance of a fever and pustules in favor of carefully recording the skin rash and the spitting of blood. Thereafter, he diagnosed the disease as caused by an abscess on the lungs.

The Romans tried to combat it with a centuries-old purification ceremony in which statues of the gods were placed on banqueting couches in public places and served with an offering. Such emotional defenses were hopelessly inadequate, so that ". . .the dead were removed [wholesale] in carts and wagons." (Julius Capitolinus, *Augustan Histories*: Marcus Antoninus XIII.2) This same source goes on to say, however, that strict laws for burial practices were introduced at this time, including one that forbade anyone from building a tomb for a plague victim at his country estate. I suspect the lives of many rural folk were saved by this constraint.

Duncan-Jones (1996) provides an excellent review of this plague episode, demonstrating the impact that the disease had on several sectors of the Roman economy including the crafts of brickmaking and quarrying of marble. In each instance, there was a dramatic decline in productivity, assuredly because of the death or flight of workers.

I also would anticipate that the plague—then truly one of the bubonic variety—which broke out at Alexandria in A.D. 250 surely damaged both the productivity of viticulture along the Nile and the ability of Alexandria to export wine to neighboring Mediterranean ports for at least a decade or so.

29 Though Pliny expressed mild respect for the wines from the Ravenna region of the northeast coast of the Adriatic, the late 1st century A.D. satirist Martial was a heavy-handed critic of them: "I would rather have a cistern at Ravenna than a vineyard, since I could sell water at a much better price." (Martial, *Epigrams* III.56); and "A crafty innkeeper cheated me the other day at Ravenna. I asked for wine and water, he sold me wine neat." (Martial, *Epigrams* III.57).

30 It is not hard to imagine the intense discussions of the relative merits of regional wines that went on during a gathering of Romans, connoisseurs or otherwise. The satirist Martial was relentless in his criticism of the wines from the Mount Vatican region that lay just beyond Rome's northwestern city limits:

> Should a god himself debit me with nectar, it would turn to vinegar and the treacherous flat content of a Vatican jar. . . . (Martial, *Epigrams* XII.48)

and

> If my little books say something smooth and agreeable, if a flattering page has a complimentary sound to it, you think this greasy fare and prefer to gnaw a rib when I give your loin of Laurentine boar. Drink Vatican if you like vinegar; my flagon doesn't suit your stomach. (Martial, *Epigrams* X.45)

and

> A serpent cased by Myron's art is on your wine bowl, Annianus, and you drink Vatican. You drink snake venum. (Martial, *Epigrams* VI.92)

Himself the owner of an estate in the countryside around Nomentum (northwest of modern Tivoli), he always wrote most fondly of wines from that region (Plate 70). His favorite wines though—apart from the traditionally renowned ones such as aged Falernian and Setine—seem to have been those from the Massic hills which separated the regions of ancient Latium and Campania near the modern town of Mondragone.

He seems to have been expressing a consensus view for his times when he wrote disparagingly of wines from the Etruscan region north of Rome: "You mix Veientan [from Veii] for me and serve Massic for yourself. I had rather smell these cups than drink." (Martial, *Epigrams* III.49). He also was quite critical of those from the Sabine hills north of Tibur (modern Tivoli) which, to the taste of his day, were regarded as harsh and acidic (Martial, *Epigrams* X.49; also Horace, *Odes and Epodes* I.20). By the late 2nd century A.D., however, the crisper, lighter Sabine and Tiburtine wines were far more respected, particularly for their medicinal qualities.

As for foreign wines, Martial could be just as disparaging—thus, of those from Egypt:

"Don't despise a jar of Nile vinegar. When it was wine, it was worse." (*Epigrams* XIII.122) He surely did not foresee the time a couple of centuries ahead when the fertility of the Campanian countryside would falter so much that Rome would choose to import appreciable amounts of Egyptian wine (see IV: A Broader Picture, and Plate 13).

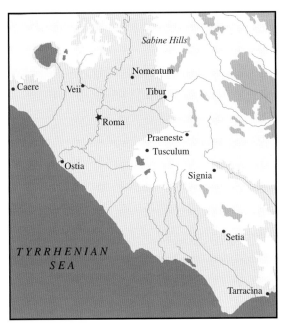

PLATE 70:

Map of the region of Italy immediately east of Rome (after Cornell and Williams [1979])

Ovidius [Martial's neighbor], when the wine that is born in the fields of Nomentum has taken to itself length of time, it sheds its character and its name with old age full of years, and the ancient jar is called whatever it desired. (Martial, *Epigrams* I.105)

31 An interesting sidebar to the story of wines enjoyed by the Roman elite is the suggestion which appears in several ancient literary sources, that the flavor and bouquet of a good vintage was improved by drinking it from a *vasa murrina*—thus: "If you drink from it hot, the murrhine suits the ardent Falernian and gives the wine a better flavor." (Martial, *Epigrams* XIV.113: see also Pliny, *Natural History* XXXVII.22) For decades, modern scholars struggled to explain this notion, until "murrhine" was identified as a fluorspar which the Romans imported from the eastern land of Parthia (see Propertius, *Elegies* IV.5). This

mineral has a relatively loose crystalline structure and chiselling it tended to cause some splintering. So, as the wine vessel took shape, it would be gently heated and smeared with a resin. This would flow into cracked areas and glue those regions together (Loewenthal and Harden 1949). Warm wine gradually would dissolve some of the resin and take up some of its sweet aroma.

32 The production of Bruttian pitch is well-documented:

> The wood of the tree [the torch pine] is chopped up and put in ovens. . .The first liquid that exudes flows like water down a pipe; in Syria this is called 'cedar juice,' and it is so strong that in Egypt it is used for embalming the bodies of the dead. The liquor that follows is thicker, and now produces pitch; this in turn is collected in copper cauldons and thickened by means of vinegar. . .and it has been given the name of Bruttian pitch. It is only useful for casks and similar receptacles, and differs from other pitch by its viscosity and also by its reddish color and because it is greasier than the rest. . .It is this pitch which is used for seasoning wine after being beaten into a powder like flour, when it has a rather black color. (Pliny, *Natural History* XVI.52)

33 Pliny claimed that certain wines while stored in wine-lofts would alter their quality at the rising of the Dog Star, but revert to their previous condition thereafter. He also credits a particular wine from the Greek island of Thasos with the ability to cure snake-bites (see *Natural History* XIV.116-118).

34 Few of Horace's poems are more famous than the one which involves Gaius Maecenas, arguably the most influential person in Octavian's life before the latter became the emperor Augustus:

> Come, drink with me—cheap Sabine, to be sure, and out of common tankards, yet wine that I with my own hand put up and sealed in a Grecian jar, on the day, dear Knight Maecenas, when such applause was paid you in the Theater that, with one accord, the banks of your native stream and the sportive echo of Mount Vatican returned your praises. Then you shall drink Caecuban and the juice of grapes crushed

by Cales' presses; my cups are flavored neither with the product of Falernum's vines nor of the Formian hills. (Horace, *Odes* I.xx)

The reader should not be surprised, however, by Horace's choice of what others would regard as a wine of only modest quality. Maecenas previously had made a gift of his Sabine estate to the poet.

35   The Romans mimicked the Greeks in so many aspects of their dining practices, not least in the habit of reclining on a couch while eating. The serving of *mulsum*, however, or indeed of any wine so early in the meal, was a distinct departure from respectable Greek traditions (Lambert-Gócs 1990).

36   The Romans were for ever harking back to their agricultural origins, with their stereotype of a humble farmer hoisting a flitch of salted bacon on his back. By the early 2nd century B.C., however, pork had shed its humble origins, and its various parts—hams, trotters, sweetbreads, tripe, etc.—had become the source of innumerable recipes for luxurious dining. (The Roman love of this meat was frequently parodied by the Latin playright, Plautus of Sarsina, in his comic depiction of the dinner parasite: see Gowers [1996].) In his *De Re Coquinaria*, the early 1st century A.D. gourmet Apicius offers dozens of pork recipes with delicately flavored herbal seasonings and sauces that were to find favor in the Roman world for centuries thereafter.

37   The determination with which Roman vintners sought to exploit the longer daylight hours of the Mediterranean region is captured well in a couple of ancient texts.

> Be the first to dig the ground, first to bear away and fire the prunings, first to carry the poles under cover; be the last to reap. (Virgil, *Georgics* II.410)

and

> Corn is crammed in every corner and many a wine jar is fragrant with ancient vintages. Here [at the villa of Faustinus], when Novembers are past and winter soon to come, the rugged pruner brings home the tardy grapes. (Martial, *Epigrams* III.58)

Ancient authors, particularly the late 1st century A.D. satirist, Martial, often refer to the famed Falernian as dark (*niger* or *fiscus*). But this most likely is a relative description, really referring to a honey-amber coloration rather than the really pale yellow one (*albus* or, paler still, *fulvus*) that we would associate with somewhat less sweet wines from the same vineyard (Fitton Brown 1962).

The finest Roman wines invariably were white because they were prepared from juices that had only brief contact with the crushed skins of the grape harvest (see *protropum* in Plate 28), irrespective of whether the grapes themselves where of a white or black variety. There were some fine dark wines in the Roman world, notably those produced on the Greek island of Thasos where the grapes were allowed to shrivel in several clusters before being processed in exactly the same way as the grapes used to make *protropum* whites. To produce red wine today, however, vintners deliberately will include the skins of black grapes in the fermentation process, extracting both their pigmentation and the tannins in them that provide the wine with an astringency which now is deemed desirable (Amerine 1964).

38   The guests at a *convivium* were not always as congenial as the name of the meal conveys to the modern ear. Petty enmities and social grudges would soon emerge as the flow of wine released inner prejudices.

> Take the case of the emperor's newly-rich freedman. He was behaving in a vulgar and pompous manner towards the philosophers who were his companions at dinner and ended by asking how it is that white beans and black alike make yellow soup. Aridices caused him to get up and leave the party mortally offended by asking in turn how it is that white and black lashes [of a whip] make red stripes. (Plutarch, *Table Talk* II.i)

Throughout early imperial literature, there is an undercurrent of distaste for freedmen (i.e., slaves released from bondage and given Roman citizenship) who thereafter gained sufficient wealth to join the higher social circles of Roman society (see, for example, Juvenal, *The Satires* III.58, VI.16 and VII.16; and Pliny, *Natural History* XXXV.58). Much of the distaste stemmed from a general distrust of foreigners that, by the very nature of the enslavement of prisoners in the wake of Roman military campaigns, the slaves invariably were. It was also sheer envy, of course, because the slaves were able to turn to fiscal advantage the administrative skills learned while managing their master's business affairs (see Petronius, *Satyricon*. 76). It often was the responsible management of the villa-based estates by such slaves, however, that ensured the success of many a famous Roman vineyard.

39   Needless to say, convivium entertainments could get out-of-hand at times. For example, it is said that at a party hosted by Mark Antony, the ex-consul Munatius Plancus danced the role of the sea-god Glaucus naked, painted blue and wearing a fish-tail as he crawled about on his hands-and-knees (Dunbabin 1996). Inevitably, the outrageous, albeit-fictitious Trimalchio, who I so often mention in this book, offered complex exhibitions throughout his convivia—among them, an acrobat who climbed a ladder held by a strong-man and then jumped through a set of burning hoops, and a group of characters who shook spears and rattled shields as they recited Greek verses, only to be followed by a mad Ajax who carved up a calf with his sword (see Petronius, *Satyricon*. 53 and 59). Such was the nature of the Roman high-life specifically in the 1st century A.D., though there is no question that such antics were equally as likely throughout all the seven centuries that the Romans dominated the Mediterranean World (Jones 1991).

40   An exchange between a convivium guest, Nigros, and his host, Aristion, gives us the gist of the opposing viewpoints on this matter.

> Nigros argued that wine should be drunk straight from the wine jar. . .purifying it like this cuts out its sinew and quenches its fire. There is a loss of bloom and dissipation of the bouquet from the repeated straining. In the second place, the practice reflects a tendency to over-refinement, vainglory and luxury, and sacrifices the useful in favor of the pleasurable. To castrate pigs and cocks, making their flesh unnaturally soft and effeminate is typical of men whose health and character are ruined by gluttony. . .and Homer somewhere. . .is accustomed to apply to wine the adjectives 'fiery-looking' (*aithops*) and 'red,' and not—as Aristion

serves it—'pale' and 'bilious-looking' from excessive purification.

Because he was comfortable with Nigros' implied criticism of soft-living Greeks and praise for traditional Roman robustness, Aristion responded with laughter.

> Not bilious-looking, my dear fellow, nor bloodless, but mellow and sunny, as appears first of all in its face. . .and you find fault with purification in terms that suggest the purging of bile; actually, it means to rid the wine of heavy, intoxicating, morbid elements and make it light in the mixture and free from anger. . . . (Plutarch, *Table Talk* VI.7)

The frequency with which wine-strainers occur in extant sets of Roman wine vessels does suggest, however, that Aristion's opinion generally prevailed (see Oliver 1977).

Charcoal was usually used as the purifying agent then as it is today, though there were other novel ideas around in those times (Gowers 1996).

> If you set Massic wine beneath a cloudless sky, all its coarseness will be toned down, and the scent, unfriendly to the nerves, will pass off; but the same wine, when strained through linen, is spoiled, losing its flavor. Surrentine wine a knowing man mixes with lees of Falernian, and carefully collects the sediment with pigeons' eggs, for the yolk sinks the bottom, carrying with it all foreign matter. (Horace, *Satires* II.iv)

41   Exquisite though some of this silverware is, the reader should realize that within the context of the Roman hierarchy of materialism, precious metals were ranked quite low. Elite drinking vessels were carved from rock crystal, amethyst, and fluorspar (see Pliny, *Natural History* XXXVII.204). Only fragments of such metal vessels remain today, however, and it is assumed that most gold vessels were melted down as bullion when taken as part of the plunders of war. Lost to us too are the precious metal cups that rich men would ornament with the jewels from their finger rings.

> The cup in [the host] Virro's hands is richly crusted with amber and rough with beryl; to you no gold is entrusted; or if it is, a watcher is posted over it to count the gems

and keep an eye on your sharp finger-nails. (Juvenal, *The Satires* V.37)

42 At the everyday level, Jewish lawmakers recognized the perils of excessive wine consumption just as well as all the Roman commentators, and they faulted its results, particularly among women, just as assertively (Broshi 1984; Dayagi-Mendels 1999).

> Do not look at wine when it is red, when it sparkles in the cup and goes down smoothly. At the last it bites like a serpent and stings like an adder. (*Proverbs* XXIII.31)

and

> One cup is becoming to a woman, two are degrading [and if she has] three she solicits publicly [but if she has four], she solicits even as an ass in the street and cares not. (*Talmud of Babylonia: Ketubot V.* folio 65a)

Within the Jewish faith, however, the notion of drunkenness prodded at far more deep-rooted emotions (Johnson 1989). Adam's temptation by Eve had been the first fall of man. But no sooner had God rid the earth of all the sons of Adam except the family of Noah than this man too fell to the first temptation he faced—his own wine (Plate 71). Wine also was the root of the incestuous downfall of the daughters of Lot.

> And the first-born said to the younger, Our father [Lot] is old, and there is not a man in the earth to come in unto us after the manner of all the earth: come, let us make our father drink wine, and we will lie with him, that we may preserve the seed of our father. . . . (*Genesis* XIX.31)

This may be why Jewish officials took a harsh line whenever drunkenness cut deeply into family harmony (see *Deuteronomy* XXI.18).

One Jewish sect, the Nazirites, preached abstinence not just from wine but from anything to do with the grape. They required of each of their adherents:

> He shall separate himself from wine and strong drink; he shall drink no vinegar of wine, or vinegar of strong drink, neither shall he drink any juice of grapes, nor eat fresh grapes or dried. All the days of his separation shall he eat nothing that is made of the grape-vine, from the kernels even to the husk. . . . (*Numbers* VI.3)

But mainstream Jewish leaders regarded wine

as a blessing, and one that helped to guide the mind to sound reasoning. Rabbis deliberately wrapped it into each important Jewish ritual—four cups to be drunk at Passover, two at weddings, just one at circumcisions, and so on.

PLATE 71:

"A Drunken Noah": detail from a 15th century A.D. French *Book of Hours*

> And the sons of Noah that went forth from the ark were Shem, and Ham, and Japheth . . .and of these was the whole earth overspread. And Noah began to be a husbandman, and planted a vineyard: and he drank of the wine, and was drunken. . . . (*Genesis* IX.20)

43 Free of guests, a loving couple might share a little wine and eat just a light meal together (Plate 72), perhaps no more than pleasantly spiced wheat wafers. A popular one was called *artoláganon*, in which the grain was blended with some wine, pepper, milk, and a small amount of olive oil (see Athenaeus, *Banquet of the Philosophers* III.113d).

Imagery for these more private moments stimulated some of the most eloquent Roman poetry over the centuries.

> I had observed which part of the cup she had touched when drinking, and then set my own lips upon that same place when I drank myself, so that as my mouth touched the brim, I seemed to send a kiss by proxy . . .Presently Satyrus once more stole away the cup and again exchanged them: then I saw her copying my action and drinking

from where I had drunk. . .and indeed for the rest of the evening we were pledging kisses to one another. (Achilles Tatius, *Leicippe and Clitophon* II.8)

PLATE 72:

"A couple relaxing with wine": detail from a 1st century A.D. wall-painting from Herculaneum

A couch for three was set out in a garden screened from view. You ask how we were placed? I was between the two. Lygdamus was in charge of the cups; there was a summer glassware service and Lesbian wine of choice vintage. (Propertius, *Elegies* IV.8)

And for the lovelorn or broken hearted:
Wine prepares the heart for love, unless you take overmuch and your spirits are dulled . . .By wind is a fire fostered, and by wind extinguished; a gentle breeze fans the flame, while a strong breeze kills it. Either no drunkenness, or so much as to banish care; aught between these two is harmful. (Ovid, *The Remedies of Love*, 805)

44   Alcaeus' poetry was much admired by late Republican writers, but only a few fragments of it survive. It is clear, however, that it often was the inspiration for imagery in the poetry of Horace. For example, there is a close match to Alceus' belief in wine as a remedy for winter's chills, in the phrase: "Dispel the chill by piling high the wood upon the hearth, and right generously bring forth in Sabine jar the wine four winters old. . . ." (Horace, *Odes* I.ix) To Alceus we owe the simple adage: "Plant no other tree than the vine." (fragment 44).

45   For example, in the mid 2nd century A.D., one *convivium* guest noted of one of his neighbors:
He was man of no worth, a trifler . . .maintaining that Plato, in his works *On the Laws*, had written most eloquently in praise of drunkenness. . .he drenched such wits as he had with frequent and large beakers, saying that it was a kind of touchwood and tinder to the intellect and the faculties, if mind and body were inflamed with wine. (Aulus Gellius, *Attic Nights* XV.3)

46   Dr. Mario Fregoni of the Viticulture Institute at the Catholic University in Piacenza recently has put forward the idea that the Romans were familiar with and enjoyed champagne as early as the latter part of the 1st century B.C. He cites as evidence a part of the description of the Caesar and Cleopatra banquet scene in Lucan's *Pharsalia* X.136-171, and a phrase "spumet et aurato mollius in calice" in:
Perish the man who discovered the heady grape and spoilt good water by mixing it with wine! . . .Let the table swim even more liberally with floods of Falernian, let it bubble more lusciously in your golden goblet. (Propertius, *Elegies* II.33b)
Readers wishing to explore this idea further, should contact Dr. Fregoni at: mfregoni@pc.unicatt.it

47   Pliny gossips a lot about the tippling of women. He noted Cato's view, for example, that the reason why women were kissed by their male relations was to know whether they smelt of *tementum* ["tipple"]. He recounts how a judge, Gnaeus Domitius, once pronounced that a certain woman had drunk more wine than was good for her health and so fined her the amount of her dowry (see *Natural History* XIV.90).
Surely the most disgusting image of a drunken woman comes from a late 1st century A.D. satire which describes the kind of wife to be avoided at all cost:
She frequents the baths at night; not till night does she order her oil flasks and her quarters to be shifted thither. . .Meanwhile her unfortunate guests are overcome with sleep and hunger, till at last she comes with a flushed face, and with thirst enough to drink dry the flagon containing a full *urna*

[half an amphora] of wine which is laid at her feet, and from which she tosses off a *sextarius* before her dinner, to create a raging appetite. Then she brings it all up again and souses the floor with the washings of her inside. The stream runs over the marble pavement; the gilt basin reeks of Falernian, for she drinks and vomits like a big snake that has tumbled into a vat. The sickened husband closes his eyes and so keeps down his bile. (Juvenal, *The Satires* VI.419)

48 Perhaps the most famous example of Roman literary character assassination of a powerful woman was that undertaken by the Greek historian, Procopius of Caesarea, against the empress Theodora (died, A.D. 548). His description of her behavior at the theater is the stuff of legends:

> . . .before the eyes of the whole people, she stripped of her clothing and moved naked through their midst, having only a girdle about her private parts and her groin . . .Clothed in this manner, she sprawled out and lay on her back on the ground. And some slaves, whose duty this was, sprinkled grains of barley over her private parts; and geese, which happen to have been provided for this very purpose, picked them off with their beaks, one by one, and ate them. And when she got up, she not only did not blush, but even acted as if she took pride in this strange performance. (Procopius, *Secret History* IX.20)

Within the context of this book, it is interesting to note that Procopius, even though he certainly loathed Theodora, and with obvious glee reveals that she was an exotic dancer and itinerant prostitute before she caught the eye of the emperor Justinian I, does not identify drunkenness among her seemingly many flaws.

49 Aristotle noted that women in his day (admittedly several centuries before such matters were the topic of any *convivium* conversation in the Roman World) tended to drink their wine in a single gulp without drawing breath. In this way the wine would not linger in them, but rather be pushed through the body by force of the draught (see Plutarch, *Table Talk* III.iii). This is an interesting thought, since we acknowledge today that sipping

through a straw, as is fashionable with certain cocktail mixes, does speed intoxication because the air drawn in with the alcohol hastens its movement into the blood stream and thereafter into the brain.

The *convivium* guest who brought up Aristotle's views on women's susceptibility to alcohol also suggested that the female body, because of a constant drawing down of fluids for menstruation, was provided with many channels. The wine could flow preferentially into these channels and so be rapidly eliminated (Plutarch, *Table Talk* III.iii). Such a notion runs contrary to the medical reality that women find themselves more affected by alcohol while ovulating or when they are premenstrual. At such times it takes the alcohol longer to be metabolized, so its concentration in the blood is higher and more prolonged (IAS 2000).

50 Besides the consequences of drunkenness, the lower efficiency with which women metabolize wine's ethanol also explains why they are more susceptible to alcoholic liver disease (see Frezza et al. 1990).

51 During both the Republican and early Imperial eras, there was a wide variety of wines available in the cities of Italy; not just those from the established vineyards of the estates encircling Rome—Setine, Falernian, Sabine, and so on (see Plates 1 and 70)—but also many imported ones from Greece and Spain. But these were rarely specified as needed by a Roman chef who, in the standard recipe books of the day, such as Apicius' *De Re Coquinaria*, would be instructed to add simply *vinum* (Solomon 1995). Whereas we might select a cooking wine for its color or for its sweetness, the Roman cook usually would use just small amounts of wine itself for such taste manipulations, instead relying just as much on unfermented grape juice (*must*) that had been pre-prepared in different ways.

For an extra touch of sweetness, there was syrupy honey-laden wine, *mulsum*, and the dark raisin wine, *passum* (see Plates 31 and 32, respectively), and for extra acidity, there was vinegar (*acetum*). For a strong wine flavor, there was the partially boiled-down must (*caroenum*) (see Plate 34); for a mild one, there was the heavily boiled-down must (*defrutum*, sometimes

A COOKED SAUCE FOR ROAST MEAT
From Apicius' *De Re Coquinaria*: recipe 270
Ingredients: Half a dozen pitted myrtle berries, cumin, pepper, honey, *garum*, olive oil, *defrutum*, and starch.
Preparation: Holding back the starch, crush all the ingredients in a casserole together with just half the *defrutum*, and cook for about ten minutes so that the sauce is partially reduced. Dissolve the starch in the rest of the *defrutum*, add this to the sauce and cook for another ten minutes. This seems to have been an all-purpose sauce for a main course of veal, venison, chicken, or pork.

PLATE 73:

"Slaves gutting a young deer for mensa prima": detail from a 1st century A.D. wall-painting

called *sapa*) (see Plates 29 and 49, and Plate 73 here). Mixtures of these various substances offered great versatility in flavors, including the ultra-sweet of *passum* plus *mulsum*, and the sweet-and-sour of *acetum* with *caroenum*, while *passum* plus *acetum* was used as a substitute for mustard. How much wine and must-derivatives were used in any particular dish has to be conjecture because these kinds of flavors are very much an acquired and individual taste. We can say though that the Romans enjoyed rich sauces on their meats, and that they had a sweet tooth when it came to desserts, so let's just say that culinary wine sometimes was used quite liberally.

It should also be remembered that the wine's flavor often would be competing with other remarkably strong ones, most obviously *garum*—the thick sauce that usually was prepared by steeping mackerel in salt along with an aromatic herbal mix—and occasionally the plantstuff *silphium*. The latter is now extinct, but it is thought to have been akin to the very pungent herb, asafetida (*ferula foetida*). Perhaps wine served to lessen some of the intensity of these other ingredients.

52   It is some measure of the size of the luxury food market in Rome that grapes themselves were preserved for year-round consumption.

Grapes of every kind can be kept without spoiling if they are plucked from the vine when the moon is waning and the weather is fine, after the fourth hour and when they have already been exposed to the sun and having no dew on them. But a fire should be made on the nearest path going from east to west, so that the pitch, in which the pedicles of the grapes may be immediately dipped, may be boiling hot. Pour an *amphora* of boiled down must [*defrutum*] into a barrel well coated with pitch; then press in cross-pieces of wood close together in such a way as not to touch the boiled down must; then put on the top new earthenware dishes and put the grapes on them in such a way that they do not touch one another; then put covers on the dishes and seal them up. Next construct another storey similarly above, and then a third, and continue the process as long as the size of the barrel allows, and arrange the grapes in the same manner. Then, after treating the lid of the barrel with pitch, smear it generously with boiled down must and then, when you have put it on, stop it up with ashes. (Columella, *On Agriculture* XII.xliv).

If that were not an elaborate enough process, Columella goes on the describe four variations of it, including one in which the grapes are put in earthenware jars that are packed mouth-down in a barrel that is then filled to the brim with the left-over mush of skins from a wine-press.

53   These humors were not mere principles. They were interwoven with the most obvious four-fold symmetry of life, Nature's four seasons (Plate 74). Phlegm, the coldest humor, increases in Winter, and so everyone sneezes and blows their running noses. Blood, increases its flow in Spring, the moist and hot season, so that is when nose-bleeds and dysenteries become common, and so on. In the 3rd century B.C., Theophrastus of Eresus asked rhetorically "Why are the unusual individuals, the men of genius, melancholics?"; and replied that in such men the black bile dominates, not just in the Fall but all the year round. Although black bile is cold and dry, hot elements intrude, and it is this mixture of cold and hot that causes the emotional instability of melancholy.

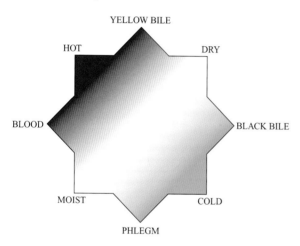

YELLOW BILE

HOT   DRY

BLOOD   BLACK BILE

MOIST   COLD

PHLEGM

PLATE 74:

The symmetry of the "humors" (after Majno 1985)
   So health of the soul means a condition when its judgments and beliefs are in harmony, and such health of soul is virtue, which some say is temperance alone, others a condition obedient to the dictates of temperance and following close upon it . . . . (Cicero, *Tusculan Disputations* IV.30)

Such concepts inevitably had to accommodate some anomalies. For example, the early 1st century A.D. physician, Cornelius Celsus, regarded wine as a "heating food," yet he spoke of vinegar as a "cooling food," in fact the coolest of them all (*On Medicine* II.27).
As with many plantstuffs, wild and cultivated, Roman doctors found practical use for almost every part of the grape vine itself. Medicinally,

the tendrils and the juice of stems of the wild vine (*Vitis sylvestris*) were drunk for dysentery and for the coughing up of blood from the lungs (*hemoptysis*), while a mash of grape skins were considered to particularly effective in cooling fevers. These same grape skins and the vine root also were used to dress leather. Late season, but still unripe grapes were fed in bunches to poultry so that "it produces in them a distaste for stealing grapes." (see Pliny, *Natural History* XIV.99). The pulped and dried skin of grapes that had been "plucked when the grapes are the size of a chick-pea, before the rising of the Dog-star" (Pliny, *Natural History* XII.131) were used to prepare *omphacium*, one of the most popular of Roman perfume ingredients.

54   The antiseptic action of wine is due to the presence of the polyphenol, malvoside, which is also the principle pigment in red wines (Majno 1975). There is a colorless equivalent in white wines. This pigment is already in the grapes, but it is combined with a carbohydrate, and so is not then an antiseptic. During the fermentation process, however, the wine's acidity allows it to split free and become active. Aging of the wine increases the amount of freed malvoside and so increases the wine's antibacterial power. But the ability for wine to heal a wound is quite limited: the active principles quickly bind to proteins in the damaged area of the skin and become inactive. Still, keeping a dressing well-soaked with wine was probably one of the more effective treatments of its day.
On the various medicinal properties of garlic (*Allium sativum*), see Block (1985).

55   Pliny, like many writers of his day, obviously subscribed to the wide-ranging power of black hellebore:

> *Nigrum* is a cure for paralysis, madness, dropsy without fever, chronic gout and diseases of the joints. It draws from the belly bile, phlegms and morbid fluids. For gently moving bowels the maximum dose is one *drachma*; a moderate one is four *oboli*. . .It matures and clears up scrofulous sores, suppurations and indurations; fistulae also, if it is taken off on the third day. With copper scales and sandarach, it removes warts. With barley meal and wine it is

applied to the abdomen for dropsy. . . . (Pliny, *Natural History* XXV.54)

Perhaps his recommendation for the various external applications had some merit. For internal treatments, however, its usage was more likely to kill the patient than many of the ailments for which it was prescribed. Hellebore's main side effects—nausea and diarrhea—often presaged death, but in terms of the "four humors" concepts of Classical medicine, such expulsion of fluids appeared highly proper and beneficial. Its only chance of working was that the vomiting which it induced might occur so rapidly that the patient got rid of the drug before absorbing a lethal dosage (Majno 1975).

Roman folklore had it that hellebore wine was produced by sowing the plant around the roots of the vine (Cato, *On Agriculture* CXIV). This wine was called *phthorium*, after a Greek word meaning "miscarriage," because it induced abortion so readily.

56 A fascinating example of this perfume/drug duality is the complex herbal mix, *kuphi*, which was said to have been concocted by Egyptian priests for a couple of thousand years before the Romans adopted it (Riddle 1985). The 1st century A.D. physician, Pedanius Dioscorides (*On Medical Matters* I.25) provided a recipe for it in Greek measures:

> half a *xestes* of nut grass (*Cyperus rotundus*) (Plate 75)
>
> half a *xestes* of ripe juniper berries (*Juniper communis*)
>
> 12 minas of plum raisins (possibly *Delphinium staphisagria*)
>
> 5 minas of purified pine resin
>
> 5 minas of sweet flag (*Acorus calamus*)
>
> 1 mina of oil of camel's thorn (*Alhagi camelorum*)
>
> 1 mina of oil of camel grass (*Cymbopogon schoenanthus*)
>
> 12 drachmas of myrrh (*Commiphora* spp.)
>
> 9 *xestai* of old wine
>
> 2 minas of honey

(Here, the *xestes* equates to the Roman *sextarius*: for U.S. and metric equivalents of the other Greek units, see XIX: Units of Capacity)

The seedless plum raisins were soaked in aged wine with myrrh along with crushed leaves of nut grass and juniper berries. This mix was blended with boiled honey and melted pine resin, and then with the oils of camel's thorn and camel grass. Though Dioscorides acknowledged *kuphi* had some medical merits—as an antidote to poison and as a drug that might relieve asthma—he observed that the Romans imported it primarily as an incense that would be used in some ritualistic way.

A similar perfume/drug duality is reflected by the up-market use of myrrh. Though one of the least scented of resins, it featured in nearly all the most sought after perfume mixes of the late Republican and early imperial eras, such as *susinum*, *cyprinum*, *megalium*, and *regale* (see Pliny, *Natural History* XIII.12-18). It would have been fair to accept the frequent mention of myrrh and other fragrant spices in ancient texts in connection with the treatment of infected wounds—for example, in Theophrastus' *On Odors*, of the 3rd century B.C.—as just a practical attempt to offset an emerging stench of putrefaction. Recent studies have shown, however, that myrrh does act as a bacteriostatic against *Staphylococcus aureus* and other gram-positive bacteria (Majno 1979). The mid 1st century A.D. physician, Dioscorides, also prescribed an aromatic wine made with balsam, myrrh, pepper, and iris, that I imagine was both quite tasty and healthy (Riddle 1985).

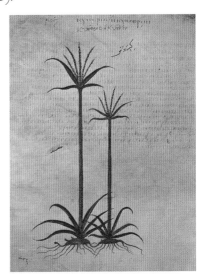

PLATE 75:

Nut grass (*Cyperus rotundus*) from Dioscorides' *De Materia Medica*

57 At all the frontiers of the Empire, a Roman soldier faced the hazard of being bitten by wild animals, snakes, or venomous insects; and in temporary encampments and war-ruined towns from which their opponents had fled, they also risked the attack of rabid dogs. Such experiences led to the development of a special line of antidotes called *theriacs*. Most of these were worthless medically, but they found a ready market among lay travelers in foreign parts. With time, theriacs also were expected to combat the murderous poisons that became such a common part of the intrigue of Roman political life (Majno 1975). In Republican times, the most popular was *Mithridatium*, which was named after its inventor, Mithridates VI of Pontus (died, 63 B.C.) (see Plate 47), and compounded thus: "two dried walnuts, two figs, and twenty leaves of rue, plus a pinch of salt. . . ." (Pliny the Elder, *Natural History* XXIII.149). Then the emperor Nero's physician, Andomachus, expanded upon this simple prescription with the dramatic addition of dozens of other ingredients, not least chunks of viper flesh, and *vini generosi quantum satis* ["as much excellent wine as is enough"]. Called thereafter *galene* ["tranquility"], it surely owed any effectiveness only to the appreciable amounts of opium included in it.

58 With their common theme of forgiveness and resurrection in death, and a meeting with the supreme deity at that time, it was difficult for erstwhile Roman pagans to truly separate the Bacchic and Christian cults from one another. So it was that the emperor Constantine's own daughter, Constantina, built her mausoleum in the church of Santa Costanza in Rome and smothered its ceiling with a mosaic of Bacchic symbols while placing herself in the scene entwined with vines.

Just as in earlier centuries pagan forces had worked so hard to hold back the growth of Christianity, so the Christian authorities strove (admittedly, less viciously) to steadily weaken the significance the Bacchic cult. An edict put out in Constantinople in A.D. 692 forbade public dancing, chorus singing, and mysteries, rating them as "the roots of all evils and ruin. . .," and "ancient customs altogether alien to Christian life. . .," respectively (see Johnson 1989). Excommunication was threatened against any vintner who might invoke the name of Bacchus while treading his grape crop or casking his wine stock.

59 The ongoing confusion between the Bacchic and Christian cults during the early Byzantine era is clear in this 5th century A.D. mosaic from Paphos in Cyprus, in which the infant wine-god is portrayed in a setting reminiscent of the *Adoration of the Magi*. Instead of the traditional maenads and satyrs, the baby Bacchus is surrounded by worshippers that include Ambrosia and Nectar, as divine food and drink, and old Tropheus the Provider (see Johnson 1989). In due time, Christianity was able to usurp several symbols of Bacchic revelry by equating the cult's emphasis on spring's fertility with the Resurrection.

60 Dreadful weather throughout that century did little to help the farmer's plight either (Dalton 1927). In A.D. 584, hailstones thrashed the early Spring vines, and then the land was consumed by a terrible drought. It is said that many angry farmers, blaming God for their misfortunes, simply laid open the gates of their vineyards and turned in the cattle and horses, thereby ensuring their ruin. The following year, famine gripped almost all of Gaul, to a point where some folk tried to feed on grass, whereupon their stomached swelled and they died. Many of the poor sold themselves into slavery for the sake of a morsel of food, while those who held grain and wine stocks indulged in blatant price-gouging. Two years later again, the vintners' problems were quite different—heavy Spring snow followed by a sharp frost, then endless torrential downpours in the Fall. The litany of grief seems near-endless.

61 Of all the monastic orders, the Cistercians were the most skilled in viticulture. The founder of their first monastery at Citeaux in A.D. 1098 was an ascetic Benedictine, Robert de Molesmes, but their inspiration was a young zealot, Bernard de Fontaine, who joined the order in A.D. 1112, and thereafter proceded to expand its influence far and wide (Johnson 1989). Under Bernard's leadership, the Cistercians revitalized the vineyards of the Côte d'Or, and they experimented there with pruning, grafting, and soil texture; they even

built walls around any fields that regularly produced a recognizable flavor. In the 12th century A.D., similar research at their abbey in the hills of the Rheingau produced a Riesling that became the white wine of choice in nearby Cologne. It is to the Cistercians that we owe the concept of a *cru*—a homogeneous section of a vineyard the wines of which prove to have an identity of quality year-in and year-out.

62   Trodden grapes produced the better quality wine of the day—*vin de goutte*. But Church estates maintained massive wine-presses that would extracted about 20% more juice from the mash brought over from a treading vat (Plate 76). This mechanization meant that *vin de presse* could be sold cheaply, but still at some significant profit (Johnson 1989). The design of this torcular press is more elaborate than the "slabs-and screw" structure commonly used in much of the Roman World (see Plate 28), but its "lever-and-screw" principle was already known to the Romans as early as the 1st century A.D. (Drachmann 1932, citing Pliny, *Natural History* XVIII.317)

PLATE 76:

"Pressing the grapes": detail from a 15th century A.D. fresco at Trento, in northeastern Italy

63   The word "eventual" in the main text was carefully chosen. All the problems of preservation that had haunted the Roman vintners were visited upon their Medieval counterparts. The grapes were trodden in a wooden trough or a shallow vat, then the juice was strained from its skins and bucketed into wooden barrels to ferment. But those barrels tended to leak, as did the ones that were used to get the wine to the marketplace. So few wines were, or could be, kept for more than a year. Some supposed experts of the day maintained that it was best to wait only long enough for the wine to complete fermentation before drinking it; this, despite the stomach upset that was likely to follow a few hours later.

Towards the end of the 15th century A.D., however, things changed, at least in the German vineyards (Johnson 1989). It was as if someone had rediscovered the ideas of Columella, Pliny, and Galen's father (see V: Legions and Legalities, and Endnotes 16 and 17) and rolled them into one, when in A.D. 1487 a royal decree was issued, permitting addition of sulfur to wine. The procedure entailed cleansing each empty barrel with the fumes of burning wood shavings that had been soaked in a mixture of powdered sulfur, herbs, and incense. Thus undesirable microbes were killed off and oxidation of the wine was suppressed; it had a much better chance both of not turning sour and of not taking on an unpleasant brown coloration. The position of German wines surely was strengthened in the marketplace by this technical advance, yet for some reason the French did not follow suit until the 18th century, at which point the newly emerging American market also recognized the error of its ways.

64   The story goes that wine prohibition came about through a chance incident when Mohammed was in exile with his disciples at Medina (Johnson 1989). One of his followers from Mecca, perhaps a little tipsy, began to recite a rude poem about the local people, at which point a Medinite snatched up a meat bone and attacked him. A distressed Mohammed asked God how he might keep his disciples in line. The reply came, "Believers, wine and games of chance, idols and divining arrows, are abominations devised by Satan. Avoid them, so that you may prosper." It is said that those present at the event were so moved that they rushed forth and poured all the wine they had into the

Medina streets.

65 Such parties could go on for days, and in literary circles, for months. Often the mental confusions of intoxication was made far worse by mixing opium with the wine (Johnson 1989). The Persians favored white wine, the Byzantines red, but both preferred sweeter varieties whatever the color. As in Roman times, it was common practice to spice wines or sweeten them to extreme with honey; and they added water in ways that were reminiscent of the rituals adopted by Athenaeus' guests at his *Banquet of the Philosophers* (see XI: A Matter of Etiquette). The greatest luxury was to mix in snow that came from the mountains or from deeply dug ice houses. This has another Roman echo here, of course: "Callistus, pour in a double double of Falernian. Alcimus, melt summer snow over it." (Martial, *Epigrams* V.64)

66 It was not that the Ottomans didn't drink, it was that they so decidely preferred the distilled spirit, *raki*—alcohol flavored with anise—and regarded it as an essential aspect of male conviviality (Johnson 1989). In the mid 17th century A.D., the Vizier Kupruli even went so far as suppress the coffee houses of Constantinople while giving privileges to that city's taverns, on the basis that the melancholy atmosphere of the former bred sedition among its clientele of politicians and poets, while the usual mood in the latter raised men's spirits to a point where thoughts of rebellion were overwhelmed by general comraderie.

67 As one might expect the Prohibition era, 1919–1933, had a chilling effect upon American wine industry. Only a few wineries kept their basic permit so that they could produce sacramental or medicinal wines. The rest were dismantled or kept closed with just a minimal attempt to maintain cooperage and equipment (Amerine 1981). After the Repeal, there was a huge demand for fortified desert wines such as muscatel and white port. These were produced rapidly, rarely aged, and sold cheaply, so there was little interest in improving grape and wine production processes or to properly time harvesting. Many years passed before normalcy returned to the industry, and better controlled vintages were laid down to mature to their current high quality.

68 According to Robinson (1999), Italian estates recently have been achieving an average wine-yield of close to 690 U.S. gallons per acre. The government statistics underlying this figure, however, identify as viticultural land as the sum of the vineyard itself—part of which would be given over to the growing of table grapes—associated vine nurseries, and some supporting general farmland (see www.agriline.it/wol). If one accepts that the vineyard represents just 40% of the estate's total land-holdings (cf. those data for ancient Settifinestre presented in Endnote 21), then the wine-yield of the typical Italian vineyard today would be more than 1730 U.S. gallons per acre. Alongside such a figure, Columella's claim that a cost-effective viticulture called for a production level of 3 *cullei* per *iugerum*—just over 660 U.S. gallons per acre (see VI: The Virtuous Vine)—seem ambitious but not outrageous.

Just then some glass jars carefully fastened with gypsum were brought on, with labels tied on their necks. . .As we were pouring over the tags, Trimalchio clapped his hands and cried, 'Ah me, so wine lives longer than miserable man. So let us be merry. Wine is life'. (Petronius, *Satyricon.* 34)

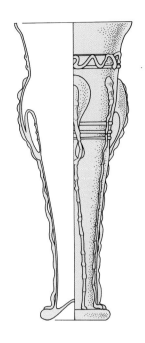

Vinneus Valens served as a captain in the Imperial guard of the late lamented Augustus; he was in the habit of holding carts laden with *cullei* up in the air until they were emptied. . . .

(Pliny, *Natural History* VII.82)

Boy, mix me *trientes* half and half, such as Pythogoras used to give to Nero, mix them, Dindymus, and not so long between them. I can do nothing sober, but when I drink, fifteen poets will come to my aid. . . .

(Martial, *Epigrams* XI.6)

Footed beaker from Flavion, Belgium
Ht., 6.9 inches
Capacity, 5.1 *cyathi*

XIX

UNITS OF CAPACITY AND MEASURE IN THE ROMAN WORLD

THROUGHOUT THE MAIN TEXT AND PLATE CAP-TIONS OF THIS BOOK, I have included several parenthetic notes on the modern equivalent of a cited Roman measurement for a capacity (dry or wet) or a weight, as much to clarify things in my own mind as to aid the reader. The conversion factors between Roman and modern units are not easy to remember. The matter is complicated by the fact that modern scholars in the main wine-producing countries of Europe reasonably enough always discuss relevant data on crop yields and consumption in metric terms (meters, liters, etc.), while writers in journals and books that cater to the American audience often present those data in what is appropriately named the U.S. System (miles, gallons, etc.). I hope that what follows will help the reader make more sense of these disparate units (see also Duncan-Jones [1982]; White [1975]; and relevant entries in the 1996 edition of *The Oxford Classical Dictionary*, pp. 942 and 1620).

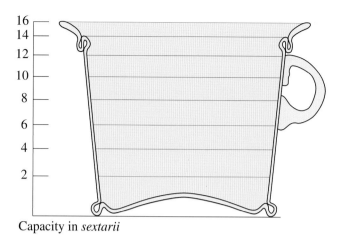

16
14
12
10
8
6
4
2

Capacity in *sextarii*

The capacity of the Roman *modius* divided into *sextarii*

STANDARDS FOR DRY AND LIQUID MEASURES
Modern conversion factors:
I U.S. gallon = 3.78 liters
I U.S. pint = 0.47 liters

Given the importance of grain in the Roman economy, it is not surprising that the grain measure (*modius*) served as the standard for dispensation of dry goods (Plate 77). According to ancient metrological sources, the Italian modius had a capacity of a third of a cubic foot, which is very close to 18.2 U.S. pints [= 8.62 liters]. There was also a *modius castrensis* which appears to have been in circulation by the mid 1st century A.D. that was then roughly equivalent to 1.36 *modii Italici* and standardized to 1.5 *modii Italici* by A.D. 301, when the emperor Diocletian issued his famous Price Edict (see Graser 1940). Fortunately, some of the confusions surrounding which modius measure is being referred to in certain ancient texts do not influence our story about Roman wine.

Whether a modius was used to measure out grain or liquids such as olive oil and wine, the standard applied was a simple one—the contents of three Italic modii would fill one amphora. Thus, one *amphora* would be equivalent to about 6.84 U.S. gallons [= 25.9 liters].

During the Republican and early Imperial eras, the *amphora* was the standard for calculating cargo burdens in the seaborne trade of wine. There were several other measures, however, that were used in both the wholesale and retail aspects of wine in the Roman economy. At one end of the scale was the *culleus*—strictly translated, the sown-up skin of an ox—which often was used as a measure for wine being carted away from a vineyard; at the other was the *cyathus* which was used as the nominal measure of the wine ladle in a tavern.

In between the culleus and the cyathus, lay the most commonly used domestic measure for both dry and wet goods—the *sextarius*—thus:
I *culleus* = 20 *amphorae*
I *amphora* = 2 *urnae* = 8 *congii*
I *congius* = 6 *sextarii*
I *sextarius* = 8 *acetabala* = 2 *heminae*
I *hemina* = 6 *cyathii*
Thus, one *sextarius* would be equivalent to a little over 0.14 U.S. gallons [= 0.54 liters].

Roman literature also refers to the *dolium*—the massive, pear-shaped jar into which the unfermented wine juice (*must*) was decanted directly from the vats of the wine press. The must was kept for about nine days in the dolium, with its mouth left open so that natural yeast spores could gain access and cause the wine to ferment. The dolium was not a standard measure, however; surviving examples range in capacity anywhere from 10 to 65 amphorae. Massive wooden casks (*cupae*) seem to have been used in much the same way as dolia and to have been just as variable in size (White 1967).

Then there was the *oenophorum* ("wine-carrier") which seems to have been a flagon about half the size of a regular amphora. In literature it usually crops up among the personal effects of travelers on long journeys over land or at sea.

One additional complication is the use of the term *keramion* meaning "jar" in trade transactions listed in Egyptian papyrii. These papyrii are our most informative source on the wholesale and retail wine prices from the 2nd century A.D. on. *Keramion* usually is translated as "amphora" in contexts where it obviously was used to store wine (for example, see Plate 9), its capacity sometimes being qualified by the adjectives *monochoron* and *dichoron*. Scholars today estimate that a *keramion monochoron* had a capacity of close to 1.9 U.S. gallons [– 7.2 liters] (Rathbone 1991).

Taverns obviously were willing and able to cater to heavy drinkers—thus:

> Phryx, a famous toper, Aulus, was blind of of one eye and bleary of the other. Heras his doctor, told him, 'Don't drink. If you drink wine, you'll lose your sight altogether.' Phryx laughs, and says to his eye 'Goodbye'; then forthwith orders *deunces* mixed for him and plenty of them. You want to know the outcome? Phryx drank wine and his eye drank poison. (Martial, *Epigrams* VI.78)

The *deunx*—strictly speaking a dry measure of 11 *unciae* (see below)—would translate here as a beaker that could hold about 7 *cyathi* or about two-thirds of a U.S. pint [= 0.31 liters]. Martial's "plenty of them" certainly would have blurred Phryx' sight, irrespective of the near-blind condition in which he entered the tavern in the first place.

STANDARDS FOR WEIGHT

Modern conversion factors:

1 U.S. pound = 454 grams
1 U.S. ounce = 28.4 grams

The standard Roman weight for dockside trade and bulkier marketplace purchases was the *libra*. Sets of such weights were recovered from Pompeii and Praenaste, in Italy, and from a shipwreck off Marseille. They indicate that one libra would be equivalent to about 0.71 U.S. pounds [= 323 grams]. Thereafter, the libra is divided into twelve *unciae*, so 1 *uncium* is equivalent to 0.95 U.S ounces [= 26.9 grams]. Herbalists putting together medicinal concoctions often used this weight, together with its finer fractions that go down to the apothe-

cary's *scripulos*, as a twenty-fourth part of an *uncium*: thus about 0.039 U.S. ounces [= 1.12 grams] (see Plate 45).

Seaborne trade in the Eastern Mediteranean frequently was carried out with the standard weight of the Greek *talent* that would be equivalent to about 57 U.S. pounds [= 25.9 kilograms] (see Plate 20). The hefty talent was broken down into more domestically relevant units—thus:

1 *talent* = 60 *minae*
1 *mina* = 100 *drachmae*
1 *drachma* = 7 *obols*.

The mina and the drachma, like the libra and the uncium, usually were used in the eastern marketplace for the sale of produce and for medicinal herbs and culinary spices: see, for example, the recipe for *kuphi* in Endnote [75].

Tying these measures together, we have:

1 *talent* = 80 *libra*
1 *mina* = 1.33 *libra*
1 *drachma* = 0.16 *uncium*

Thus, a *drachma* is equivalent to 0.15 U.S. ounces [= 4.31 grams].

STANDARDS FOR AREAS

Modern conversion factors:

1 mile = 1.61 kilometers
1 inch = 2.54 centimeters
1 acre = 0.00156 square miles = 4047 square meters

The Roman foot (*pes*) is estimated to be equivalent to about 11.65 inches or 29.6 centimeters. For longer distances we have:

1 Roman mile = 1,000 *passi*
1 *stadium* = 125 *passi*
1 *passus* [pace] = 5 *pedes*

For areas, the Romans employed the *actus quadratus*—a square of 120 pes—two of which formed an *iugerum*. Thus, the *iugerum* is equivalent to about 0.62 acres or 2,500 square meters.

Within the context of Roman wine yields, it is worth repeating the most important estimate made in the main text—that 1 *culleus* per *iugerum* is equivalent to 220 U.S. gallons per acre.

It has pleased us to engrave scenes of licence upon our goblets, and to drink through the midst of obscenities."

(Pliny, *Natural History* XXXIII.5)

. . .vines having the remarkable property of drawing into themselves the flavor of some other plant, which explains why the grapes plucked in the marshes of Padua actually have the flavor of willow.

(Pliny, *Natural History* XIV.110)

"Pliny offering his texts to the emperor Titus": vignette from the early 13th century A.D. *Codex Plutarch*

XX

SOURCES, ANCIENT AND MODERN

QUOTATIONS MARKED AS CIL, ILS AND ILLRP ARE FROM THE STANDARD WORKS: *Corpus Inscriptionum Latinarum* (initiated in 1863 and still being updated); *Inscriptiones Latinae Selectae* (edited by H. Dessau and published 1892-1916); and *Inscriptiones Latinae Liberae Rei Publicae* (edited by A. Degrassi, initiated in 1963 and still being extended). Statistics for modern wine production and consumption (including alcoholism) are drawn from *The Oxford Companion to Wine* by Jancis Robinson (1999), appendix 2; and from several current Websites, including:

agriline.it
alcoweb.com
census.gov/ipc
cocktails.miningco.com
faculty.biu.ac.il/~barilm/infant
ias.org.uk/factsheets
photius.com
wineinstitute.org

The following ancient writers are cited most frequently in the text, endnotes, and plate captions of this book. Details of their lives are drawn primarily from *The Oxford Classical Dictionary* edited by Simon Hornblower and Antony Spawforth (1996).

• Apicius [Marcus Gavius Apicius]: early 1st century A.D.

Little is known about this gourmet, except that he was a notorious resident of the resort of Minturnae (modern Minturno) on the Bay of Naples and that he claimed to have inspired the notion of an "eating-house cuisine" (*scientia popinae*). *De Re Coquinaria*, the collection of recipes that bears his name, is now thought to have been compiled in the 4th century A.D. Whatever the truth of authorship may be, those recipes give us a detailed insight into the diverse use of wine in Roman culinary arts.

Later writers claim that he would have been a wealthy man except for his taste in luxury foods, particularly crayfish. Imagining that one day he would be poor and unable to support his gourmet pleasures, he arranged a banquet in honor of his skills and, with the foreknowledge of his guests, committed suicide by poison (see Seneca, *Consolation for Helvia* X.8).

• Athenaeus: active, circa A.D. 200

Little is known of this writer's life, other than he was from Naucratis in Egypt. His multi-volumed *Banquet of the Philosophers*—fifteen books are extant, but originally it may have been twice that size—stands today as a remarkable compendium of earlier great writers whose beliefs are artfully woven into the conversation of an imaginary Roman *convivium*. It is an excellent resource for comparing and contrasting Greek and Roman views of wine.

• Cato [Marius Porcius Cato]: 234–149 B.C.

He was born at Tusculum (modern Frascati, southeast of Rome: see Plate 70), but spent much of his childhood in the Sabine hills where his family owned land. Cato became a dominant figure in both the political and cultural life of Rome during the first half of the 2nd century B.C., perhaps being remembered most in his own times for his intense antagonism to all things Greek: Columella (*On Agriculture* I.I) observed that "Cato first taught agriculture to speak Latin." But Cato's *On Agriculture* is concerned less with agricultural practice as a whole, than with advising owners of mid-sized estates in Latium or Campania how best to manage their slave work-force—in practice, quite ruthlessly—and how to market their primary produce which in his day was wine and olives.

• Cicero [Marcus Tullius Cicero]: 106–43 B.C. (see the heading for V: Legions and Legalities)

He was born at Arpinum (modern Arpino, in the hills of Latium), and educated in philosophy and rhetoric in Rome and later in Greece. By 80 B.C., despite his youth, he had emerged as the preeminent lawyer in Rome. During the subsequent two decades, he secured some surprising convictions for corruption among State officials, and defended many highly placed patricians who found themselves at odds with the prevalent political mood (see Plate 16, in connection with the trial of Marcus Fonteius). His openly expressed admiration for Sulla cost him dearly, however, as Julius Caesar's power steadily rose to dictatorship. As a consequence and through some subtle legal manipulations in the Senate, he was forced into a year-long exile in 58 B.C. Thereafter his career experienced several reversals—some of them contrived by his political enemies—so he eventually withdrew from the then collapsing world of Republican politics, preferring instead to concentrate more on writing treatises on rhetoric, such as *On Oratory* (55 B.C.), and on philosophic issues and morality, such as *On Duties* (44 B.C.). The sixteen books of his personal correspondence with family members, friends, and colleagues that were published after his death—particularly *Letters to Atticus*—have proven to be one of the richest resources for understanding the historical events and social life of his time.

• Columella [Lucius Junius Moderatus Columella]: ?—circa A.D. 70

Although he was born at Gades (modern Cadiz) in Spain, Columella spent the greater part of his life on farms that he owned in the vicinity of Rome. His twelve-book *On Agriculture* is the most systematic work on the details of Roman agricultural practice that we have. The farm called Ceretanum, upon which Columella seems to have based many of his observations about wine yields and the planning of viticulture, probably was located near Caere (modern Cerveteri) in Etruria.

• Horace [Quintus Horatius Flaccus]: 65–8 B.C.

He was born at Venusia (modern Venosa) in the Apulia region of southeastern Italy. Like many affluent young Romans, he went to Athens to complete his education in philosophy. After just two years there, however, his studies were interrupted by poiltical events. He took the unfortunate step of throwing in his lot with the senator Brutus just before the latter was soundly defeated by Octavian—emperor-to-be Augustus—at the battle of Philippi. Taking advantage of the general amnesty granted by Octavian, he returned to Rome in 41 B.C., thereafter to develop friendship with nearly all the eminent Romans of his time. His poetry, published variously as Epodes, Satires, and Odes, contains innumerable allusions to the pleasures of drinking wine, many of which are included in this book. He owned a fine vine-growing estate in the Sabine Hills northeast of Rome (see Endnote 34, and Plate 70).

• Juvenal [Decimus Iunius Iuvenalis]: ?—A.D. 140

Little of his private life is known, except that he was born at Aquinum (modern Aquino, in the hills of Latium). His writings, however, are among the most quoted today (not least by myself) in any discussion of the social structure of early imperial Roman life. Of his *The Satires*, the first nine books are a scathing criticism of so many things Roman, with frequent attacks on the dead rather than the living, and a relentless attack on the morals of the wealthy and their insensitivity to the plight of the poor. The remaining seven books have a quite different, less personal tone. They cover topics such as frugal eating, the futility of prayer, and the problems of a guilty conscience.

Perhaps he will best be remembered for the quotations, *mens sana in corpore sano* ["a healthy mind in a healthy body"] and *quis custodiet ipsos custodes?* ["who guards the guards themselves?"].

• Martial [Marcus Valerius Martialis]: circa A.D. 41–104

He was born at Bilbilis (modern Calatayud) in Spain and moved to Rome in A.D. 64. There he was supported by several patrons, including the younger Seneca, who was then the most celebrated Spaniard in the city. His fourteen books of *Epigrams* capture, albeit sometimes quite obscenely, the entire spirit of Roman life, both private and public. Though all his characters are fictitious, one senses that they are

drawn from real people that he encountered from all walks of life—the street-hawker and the charlatan doctor; the politically skilled prostitute and the selfish dinner host. His own love of "the good life" and some signs of connoiseurship in matters of wine is why his writings feature so strongly in this book.

• Petronius [Gaius Petronius Arbiter]: ?—A.D. 66

Nothing is known about this writer's early life, but he emerges during the reign of the emperor Claudius as a man of pleasure and good literary taste. As the historian Tacitus describes him, he used to sleep by day and attend to official duties or to his amusements by night. Though he held some political appointments, in later life he lapsed into indulgence, becoming a close friend of the emperor Nero. In A.D. 66. however, accused of disloyalty and condemned, it is said that he sat with self-opened veins bandaged and chatted lightly with friends, dined and drowsed, and then, before he died, had the temerity to send the Nero a survey of that emperor's sexual excesses.

His *Satyricon* is a mix of philosophy and real life held together by a fictitious story. For the most part, the story itself is played out by a rich freedman, Trimalchio, and a number of disreputable dinner guests. The text is littered with deliberate excess and bad taste. For example, at one point Trimalchio asks for his grave-clothes and wraps himself in the winding-sheet. According to one guest:

> The thing was becoming perfectly sickening, when Trimalchio, now deep in the most vile drunkenness, had a new set of performers, some trumpeters, brought into the dining-room, propped himself on a heap of cushions and stretched himself on his death-bed, saying, 'Imagine that I am dead. Play something pretty.' (*Satyricon*, 78).

Frequent mention of Trimalchio's activities in this book reflect the fact that he was so often either drunk or talking about being so.

• Pliny [Gaius Plinius Secundus]: A.D. 23–79

He was born at Novum Comum (modern Como) in the Lombardia region of northeastern Italy. Under the emperor Vespasian, he pursued a career that was partly military in the Rhineland and partly administrative in Gaul and Spain. Eventually, he became commander of the fleet at Misenum (modern Miseno) on the northern tip of the Bay of Naples. When Mt. Vesuvius erupted on August 24, A.D. 79, duty and curiosity combined, fatally; he led a detachment to the disaster area and died from inhaling the volcano's sulfurous fumes. That event apart, he is best known for his encyclopaedic thirty-seven book *Natural History*, from which I have quoted on innumerable occasions in this book. His writing covers all contemporary knowledge—animal, vegetable, and mineral—but with much that is human too, including ghosts and other supernatural phenomena given credence in his day. His writings often are quite pedantic. For my part, however, I think of him as someone who could not resist, once in a while, taking the opportunity within his scholarly script to rail at medical charlatans and at the nouveau-riche or politically successful freedmen , all of whom he regarded as upstarts within the mood of a Republican revival that was strong in his times.

• Plutarch [Mestrius Plutarchus]: circa A.D. 50–120

He was born at Chaeronea (north of modern Levadhia) in central Greece, and spent most of his life in that town. In his writings, he was a strong exponent of the concept of a partnership between Greece, the educator, and Rome, the great power; something that sat well with the emperor Hadrian, who thought of himself as a later-day Athenian philosopher. Plutarch was a prolific writer, but it was his *Parallel Lives* and his *Table Talk* that best stood the test of time, both being popular educational texts during the Byzantine era. The latter, which was written after the murder of the emperor Commodus in A.D. 193, is full of social commentary and curious speculation, and is key to our understanding of many aspects wine's role in elite Roman society.

• Suetonius [Gaius Suetonius Tranquillus]: circa A.D.70–130

He was born at Hippo Regius (modern Annaba) in North Africa, but corresondence with Pliny the Younger indicates that was already attract-

ing attention in Rome as a scholar by about A.D. 97. His twelve-book *Lives of the Caesars* is a set of biographies which include Julius Caesar and the successive emperors from Augustus to Domitian. He became the emperor Hadrian's private secretary in A.D. 119 but was dismissed just two years later, seemingly for a breach of court etiquette. It is thought that, in this forced retirement, he wrote a great deal, but only a part of his *Lives of Illustrious Men* survive from that time. Perhaps he is best known for his acount of Nero's death (*Lives of the Caesars* VI.xlv–xlix).

• Varro [Marcus Terentius Varro]: 116-27 B.C.

He was born at Reate (modern Riati) in the Sabine hills northeast of Rome. Study in Rome and Athens prepared him for a public career that eventually placed him in the service of the Pompeian side in the Civil War. The subsequent clemency granted him by Julius Caesar allowed him to plan Rome's first public library, but Caesar's assassination resulted in his proscription. In forced retirement and scholarly seclusion, he wrote prolifically, including the three book *On Agriculture* of 37 B.C. frequently quoted in this book. As a treatise on farming, it is presented in dialogue form, and seems intended to be something of an entertainment for men of Varro's own class. The treatise often reveals a cruel streak in his character—though one that we have to accept was close to the norm for his day—slaves being labeled as instruments, separated from cattle for that purpose only by virtue of the fact that they could speak (*On Agriculture* I.xvii).

The Oxford Classical Dictionary cited earlier is also a source for the careers of Greek and Roman writers mentioned in passing in the main text and the endnotes (or are directly referenced in the translations listed below), such as Aeschylus of Eleusis, Aristotle of Stagira, Livy of Patavium, Lucian of Samosata, Ovid of Sulmo, Plautus of Sarsina, Polybius of Megalopolis, Procopius of Caesarea, Tacitus of Narbonne, Theomompus of Chios, and Theophrastus of Eresus.

TRANSLATIONS AND COMMENTARIES

Ash, H.B., 1993: *Columella: On Agriculture*, Books I–V (Cambridge: Harvard University).

Atwater, R., 1966: *Procopius' Secret History* (Ann Arbor: University of Michigan).

Bennett, C.E., 1918: *Horace: The Odes and Epodes* (Cambridge: Harvard University).

Cameron, A., 1976: *Flavius Cresconius Corippus: In laudem Iustini Augusti minoris* IV (London: Athlone).

Clement, P.A. and Hoffleit, H.B., 1969: *Plutarch's Moralia* VIII (Cambridge: Harvard University).

Cahon, J.W., 1985: *Dio Chrysostom* II (Cambridge: Harvard University).

Cole, F.C., 1971: *Plutarch's Moralia* II (Cambridge: Harvard University).

Cornish, F.W., 1962: *The Poems of Catullus* (Cambridge: Harvard University).

Dalton, G.M., 1927: *The History of the Franks by Gregory of Tours* (Oxford: Clarendon).

Forster, E.S. and Heffner, E.H., 1993: *Columella: On Agriculture*, Books X–XII (Cambridge: Harvard University).

Gaselee, S., 1947: *Apuleius: The Golden Ass* (Cambridge: Harvard University).

Giacosa, I.G., 1992: *A Taste of Ancient Rome* (Chicago: University of Chicago).

Goold, G.P., 1990: *Propertius: Elegies* (Cambridge: Harvard University).

Gulick, C.B., 1969: *Athenaeus: The Deipnosophists* IV (Cambridge: Harvard University).

Hooper, W.D., 1999: *Marcus Porcius Cato: On Agriculture and Marcus Terentius Varro: On Agriculture* (Cambridge: Harvard University).

Jones, W.H.S., 1989: *Pliny: Natural History*, Books XX–XXIII (Cambridge: Harvard University).

Jones, W.H.S., 1992: *Pliny: Natural History*, Books XXIV–XXVII (Cambridge: Harvard University).

Minar, E.L., Jr., Sandbach, F.H. and Helmbold, W.C., 1969: *Plutarch's Moralia* IX (Cambridge: Harvard University).

Neusner, J., 1988: *The Mishnah* (New Haven: Yale University).

Neusner, J., 1992: *The Talmud of Babylonia* XIV.B: Tractate Ketubot, and XXII.C: Tractate Baba Batra (Atlanta: Scholars).

Rackham, H., 1986: *Pliny: Natural History*, Books XII–XVI (Cambridge: Harvard University).

Rackham, H., 1992: *Pliny: Natural History*, Books XVII–XIX (Cambridge: Harvard University).

Rackham, H., 1995: *Pliny: Natural History*, Books XXXIII–XXXV (Cambridge: Harvard University).

Radice, B., 1969: *Pliny: Letters*: Books VIII-X (Cambridge: Harvard University).

Ramsey, G.G., 1996: *Juvenal and Persius* (Cambridge: Harvard University).

Rieu, E.V., 1946: *Homer: The Odyssey* (Baltimore: Penguin).

Rolfe, J.C., 1928: *The Attic Nights of Aulus Gellius* III (New York: Putnam).

Rolfe, J.C., 1989–92: *Suetonius* I and II (Cambridge: Harvard University).

Shackleton Bailey, D.R., 1993: *Martial: Epigrams* I–III (Cambridge: Harvard University).

Spencer, W.G., 1971: *Celsus: De Medicina* I–III (Cambridge: Harvard University).

O'Sullivan, J.H., 1947: *The Writings of Salvian the Presbyter* (New York: Cima).

Van Dam, R., 1988: *Gregory of Tours: Glory of the Confessors* (Liverpool: Liverpool University).

Warmington, E.H., 1987: *Petronius: Satyricon* (Cambridge: Harvard University).

Watts, N.H., 1979: *Cicero* XIV: Pro M. Fonteio (Cambridge: Harvard University).

Watson, A., 1985: *The Digest of Justinian* III (Philadelphia: University of Pennsylvania).

Winstedt, E.O., 1967: *Cicero*: Letters to Atticus (Cambridge: Harvard University).

The saying 'I dislike a drinking companion with a good memory' some say, my dear Sossius Senecio, was meant by its author to refer to masters of ceremonies who are rather tiresome men and wanting in taste when the drinking is on. . .some think the proverb recommends amnesty for all that is said and done during the drinking. . . .

(Plutarch, *Table Talk* I.i)

"A Leper drinking wine": detail for November from the 9th century A.D. *Calendar of Wandalbert–Matyrgiums*

XXI

REFERENCES

Ahlström, G.W., 1978: "Wine presses and cup-marks of the Jenin-Megiddo survey," *Bulletin of the American Schools of Oriental Research* 231, 19-49.

Amerine, M.A., 1964: "Wine," *Scientific American* 211.2, 2-12.

Amerine, M.A., 1981: "Development of the American wine industry to 1960," in *Wine Production Technology in the United States*, 1-28 (edit., M.A. Amerine; Washington DC: American Chemical Society).

Aubert, J.-J., 1994: *Business Managers in Ancient Rome*, 162-171 and 265-276 (New York: E.J. Brill).

Bagnall, R.S. and Frier, B.W., 1994: *The Demography of Roman Egypt*, 75-110 (New York: Cambridge University).

Baines, J. and Málek, J., 1980: *Atlas of Ancient Egypt*, 25 (New York: Facts on File).

Bell, H.I., 1924: *Jews and Christians in Egypt*, papyrus 1915 (London: Oxford University).

Broshi, M., 1984: "Wine in ancient Palestine: introductory notes," *Israel Museum Journal* III, 21-40.

Baratte, F., 1989: "La verrerie dans l'Afrique Romaine: état des questions," *Kölner Jahrbuch für Vor- und Frühgeschichte* 22, 141–149.

Block, E., 1985: "The chemistry of garlic and onions," *Scientific American* 252.3, 114-119.

Callender, M.H., 1965: *Roman Amphorae with Index of Stamps*, various entries (London: Oxford University).

Carandini, A., 1980: "Il vignito e la villa del fondo di Settefinestre nel Cosano: un caso di produzione agricola per il mercato transmarino," *Memoirs of the American Academy in Rome* XXXVI, 1-10.

Carandini, A., 1983: "Columella's vineyard and the rationality of the Roman economy," *Opus* 2, 177-204.

Carandini, A. and Panella, C., 1981: "The trading connections of Rome and Central Italy in the late second and third centuries: the evidence of the Terme del Nuotatore excavations, Ostia," in *The Roman West in the Third Century*, 487-503 (edits., A. King and M. Henig; Oxford: BAR Intern. Series 109).

Casson, L., 1979: *The "Periplus Maris Erithraei,"* 11–39 (Princeton: Princeton University).

Casson, L., 1990: "New light on maritime loans: P. Vindob G 40822," *Zeitscrift für Papyrologie und Epigraphik* 84, 195-206.

Cockle, H., 1981: "Pottery manufacture in Roman Egypt: a new papyrus," *Journal of Roman Studies* 71, 87-97.

Chadwick, H. and Evans, G.R., 1989: *Atlas of the Christian Church*, 24-35 (New York: Facts on File).

Cornell, T. and Williams, J., 1983: *Atlas of the Roman World*, 20, 129, and 157 (New York: Facts on File).

Dalby, A. and Grainger, S., 1996: *The Classical Cookbook*, 90 and 109-111 (Malibu: The J. Paul Getty Museum).

Dar, S. (edit.), 1999: *Sumaqa: a Roman and Byzantine Jewish Village on Mount Carmel, Israel*, 95-107 (Oxford: BAR Intern. Series 815).

D'Arms, J.H., 1981, *Commerce and Social Standing in Ancient Rome*, 48-71 and 97-120 (Cambridge: Harvard University).

Davis, L., 1999: *Two for the Lions*, 154-155 (New York: Warner).

Davies, R.W., 1970: "Some Roman medicine," *Medical History* XIV, 101-106.

Dayagi-Mendels, M., 1999: *Drink and Be Merry*, 39-51 (Jerusalem: The Israel Museum).

Drachmann, A.G., 1932: "Ancient oil mills and presses," *Archaeologisk-kunsthistoriske Meddelelser* I.I, 50-63 and figures 12-17.

Dunbabin, K.M.D., 1993: "Wine and water in the Roman convivium," *Journal of Roman Archaeology* 6, 116-141.

Dunbabin, K.M.D., 1996: "Convivial spaces: dining and entertainment in the Roman villa," *Journal of Roman Archaeology* 9, 66-80.

Duncan-Jones, R., 1982: *The Economy of the Roman Empire*, 369-372 (New York: Cambridge University).

Duncan-Jones, R., 1996: "The impact of the Antonine plague," *Journal of Roman Archaeology* 96, 108-136.

Egloff, M., 1977: *Kellia: la Poterie Copte*, various plates (Geneva: Georg).

Eisinger, J., 1996: "Sweet poison," *Natural History* 105.7: 48-53.

Fitton Brown, A.D., 1962: "Black wine," *Classical Review* 12, 192-195.

Fleming, S.J., 1997: *Roman Glass: Reflections of Everyday Life*, 52-59 (Philadelphia: University of Pennsylvania Museum).

Fleming, S.J., 1999: *Roman Glass: Reflections on Cultural Change*, 62-66 (Philadelphia: University of Pennsylvania Museum).

Frezza, M. et al., 1990: "High blood alcohol levels in women: the role of decreasd gastric consumption. Alcohol dehydrogenase and first-pass metabolism," *New England Journal of Medicine* 322.2, 95-99.

Frier, B.C., 1983: "Roman law and the wine trade: the problem of 'vinegar sold as wine'," *Zeitschrift der Savigny-Stiftung für Rechsgeschichte* 100, 257-295.

Fuks, A., 1951: "Notes on the archive of Nicanor," *Journal of Juristic Papyrology* V, 207-216.

Galliou, P., 1981: "Western Gaul in the third century," in *The Roman West in the Third Century*, Part II, 259-286 (edits., A King and M. Henig; Oxford: BAR Intern. Series 109).

Geremek, H., 1971: "P. Iandana 99: Italian wines in Egypt," *Journal of Juristic Papyrology* 16/17, 159-171.

Giacosa, I.G., 1992: *A Taste of Ancient Rome*, various entries (Chicago: University of Chicago).

Goethert-Polaschek, K., 1977: *Katalog der römischen Gläser des Rheinischen Landesmuseums Trier*, various entries (Mainz: Phillipp von Zabern).

Goudineau, C., 1983: "Marseilles, Rome, and Gaul from the third to the first century B.C.," in *Trade in the Ancient Economy*, 76-86 (edits., P.D.A. Garnsey, K. Hopkins and C.R. Whittaker; Berkeley: University of California).

Gowers, E., 1996: *The Loaded Table*, 66-76 (Oxford: Clarendon).

Graser, E.R., 1940: "Appendix: The Diocletian Edict," in *An Economic Survey of Ancient Rome, Part V*, 305-421 (London: Oxford University).

Greene, K., 1978: "Roman trade between Britain and the Rhine provinces: the evidence of pottery to c. A.D. 250," in *Roman Shipping and Trade: Britain and the Rhine Provinces*, 58-68 (edits., J. du Plat Taylor and H. Cleere; London: Council for British Archaeology).

Grenfell, B.P. Hunt, A.S. and Bell, H.I., 1924: *The Oxyrhynchus Papyri XVI*, entry 2046 (London: Egypt Exploration Society).

Greene, K., 1986: *The Archaeology of the Roman Economy*, 156-168 (Berkeley: University of California).

Harden, D.B., 1987: *Glass of the Caesars*, entries 70, 104, 119 and 139 (Milan: Olivetti).

Harris, W.V., 1993: "Between archaic and modern: some current problems in the history of the Roman economy," in *The Inscribed Economy*, 9-29 (edit., W.V. Harris; Ann Arbor: University of Michigan).

Hitchner, R.B., 1992: "Meridional Gaul, trade and the Mediterranean economy in late antiquity," in *Fifth Century Gaul: A Crisis of Identity?*, 122-143 (edits., J. Drinkwater and H. Elton; New York: Cambridge University).

Hunt, E.D., 1982: *Holy Pilgrimage in the Later Roman Empire A.D. 312–460*, 1-43 (Oxford: Clarendon).

IAS, 2000: Istitute of Alcohol Studies factsheets via the Website www.ias.org.uk.

Jackson, R., 1988: *Doctors and Diseases in the Roman Empire*, various entries (Norman: University of Oklahoma).

Jashemski, W.F., 1973: "Large vineyard discovered in ancient Pompeii," *Science* 180: 821-830.

Johnson, H., 1989: *Vintage: The Story of Wine*, various entries (New York: Simon and Schuster).

Jones, C.P., 1991: "Dinner theater," in *Dining in a Clasical Context*, 185-198 (edit., W.J. Slater; Ann Arbor: University of Michigan),

King, A., 1990: *Roman Gaul and Germany*, 189-201 (Berkeley: University of California).

Kondoleon, C., 2000; "Mosaics of Antioch," in *Antioch: The Lost Ancient City*, 63-77 (edit., C. Kondoleon; Princeton: Princeton University).

Lambert-Gócs, M., 1990: *The Wines of Greece*, 252-291 (Boston: Faber and Faber).

Leclant, J., 1973: "Glass from the Meroitic necropolis of Sedeinga (Sudanese Nubia)," *Journal of Glass Studies* 15: 52–68.

A.Y. Leung, 1980: *Encyclopaedia of Common Natural Ingredients*, various entries (New York: John Wiley).

Levick, B., 1982: "Domitian and the provinces," *Latomus* 41, 50-73.

Liou, B. and Pomey, P., 1985: "Direction des recherches archéologiques sous-marines," *Gallia* 43, 547-576.

Loewental, A.I. and Harden, D.B., 1949: "Vasa murrina," *Journal of Roman Studies* XXXIX, 31-37.

MacMullen, R., 1988: *Corruption and the Decline of Rome*, 21-35 (New Haven: Yale University).

Majno, G., 1975: *The Healing Hand*, 186-190 and 414-416 (Cambridge: Harvard University).

Mattingly, D.J., 1988: "Oil for export?: a comparison of Libyan, Spanish and Tunisian olive oil production in the Roman Empire," *Journal of Roman Archaeology* I, 33-56.

Mayerson, P., 1985: "The wine and vineyards of Gaza in the Byzantine period," *Bulletin of the American Schools of Oriental Research* 257, 75-80.

Mayerson, P., 1993: "The use of Ascalon wine in the medical writers of the fourth to the seventh centuries," *Israel Exploration Journal* 43, 169-173.

Middleton, P., 1983: "The Roman army and long distance trade," in *Trade and Famine in Classical Antiquity*, 75-83 (edits., P.D.A Garnsey and C.R. Whittaker; Berkeley: University of California).

Moevs, M.T.M., 1973: "The Roman thin-walled pottery from Cosa," *Memoirs of the American Academy in Rome* XXXI-II, 49-58.

Nutton, V. 1969: "Medicine and the Roman army: a further reconsideration," *Medical History* 13.3, 260-270.

Oliver, A. Jr., 1977: *Silver for the Gods*, 126-131 (Toledo: Toledo Museum of Art).

Parker, A.J., 1992: "Cargoes, containers and stowage: the ancient Mediterranean," *The International Journal of Nautrical Archaeology* 21.2: 89-100.

Peacock, D.P.S. and Williams, D.F., 1986: *Amphorae and the Roman Economy*, various entries (New York: Longman).

Potter, T.W., 1990: *Roman Italy*, various entries (Berkeley: University of California).

Rathbone, D.W., 1981: "The development of agriculture in the *Ager Cosanus* during the Roman Republic: problems of evidence and interpretation," *Journal of Roman Studies* 71, 10-23.

Rathbone, D.W., 1983: "Italian wines in Roman Egypt," *Opus* II, 81-98.

Raven, S., 1993: *Rome in Africa*, 79–99 and 132–143 (New York: Routledge).

Riddle, J.M., 1985: *Dioscorides on Pharmacy and Medicine*, 142-146 (Austin: University of Texas).

Riddle, J.M., 1997: *Eve's Herbs*, 35-63 (Cambridge: Harvard University).

Rickman, G.E., 1971: *Roman Granaries and Store Buildings*, 73-76 (New York: Cambridge University).

Robinson, J., 1999: *The Oxford Companion to Wine*, Appendix 2 (New York: Oxford University).

Roll, I. and Ayalon, E., 1981: "Two large wine presses in the red soil regions of Israel," *Palestine Exploration Quarterly* 113, 111-125.

Rossiter, J.J., 1981: "Wine and oil processing at Roman farms in Italy," *Phoenix* 35, 345-361.

Scarborough, J., 1996: "Drugs and medicines in the Roman World," *Expedition* 38.2, 39-51.

C. Scarre, 1995: *Chronicle of the Roman Emperors*, 148-153 (New York: Thames and Hudson).

Scobie, A., 1986: "Slums, sanitation, and mortality in the Roman World," *Klio* 68, 399-433.

J.-A. Shelton, 1988: *As the Romans Did*, 168-189 (New York: Oxford University).

Solomon, J., 1995: "The Apician sauce," in *Food in Antiquity*, section II.9 (edits., J. Wilkins, D. Harvey and M. Dobson; Exeter: Exeter University).

Stuart, M. (edit.), 1979: *The Encyclopaedia of Herbs and Herbalism*, various entries (New York: Grosset and Dunlap).

Tait, J.G., 1930: *Greek Ostraca in the Bodleian Library at Oxford* I, entry 240 (London: Egypt Exploration Society).

Tchernia, A., 1983: "Italian wine in Gaul at the end of the Republic," in *Trade in the Ancient Economy*, 87-104 (edits., P.D.A Garnsey, K. Hopkins and C.R. Whittaker: Berkeley; University of California).

Tchernia, A., 1986: *Le Vin de Italie Romaine*, Appendix II (Rome: École Francais).

Vickers, M., 1996: "Rock crystal: the key to cut glass and *diatreta* in Persia and Rome," *Journal of Roman Archaeology* 9, 48-65.

Wagner, P., 1974: "Wines, grape vines and climate," *Scientific American* 230.6: 106-115.

Watson, A. (transl.), 1985: *The Digest of Justinian* III, book 33.6 (Philadelphia: University of Pennsylvania).

Weinberg, G.D., 1985: *Excavations at Jalame*, 38-102 (Columbia: University of Missouri).

White, K.D., 1967: *Farm Equipment of the Roman World*, various entries (New York: Cambridge University).

Wilkinson, J., 1977: *Jerusalem Pilgrims before the Crusades*, 1-15 (Warminster: Aris and Phillips).

INDEX

ABOUT THE AUTHOR

I was born and raised in South Wales. My father was an amateur artist, so my brother and I often would spend weekend afternoons clambering over the remains of Roman camps while he captured the charm of nearby villages in and around the Wye valley. I was brought up among tales of how the woad-painted native peoples, the Silures, fiercely defended their homeland and held at bay the advancing Roman legions, despite their superior weaponry. So it has been fascinating for me to come full circle, after a thirty-year career in physics and archaeology, and take a fresh look at the Romans via a socially refined aspect of their culture rather than revive my youthful memories of their militancy.

I received my first degree and my doctorate from Oxford University, specializing in radiation damage processes in minerals and their potential for the dating of ancient pottery. In 1978, I took up my current position of Scientific Director for the Museum Applied Science Center for Archaeology (MASCA) at the University of Pennsylvania Museum. I am the author of five books: *Authenticity in Art* (1975), *Dating in Archaeology* (1976), *Thermoluminescence Dating in Archaeology* (1979), *The Egyptian Mummy: Secrets and Science* (1981), *Roman Glass: Reflections of Everyday Life* (1997), and most recently, *Roman Glass: Reflections on Cultural Change* (1999). It was the dynamic cultural story underlying the last of these books that inspired me to tackle the some-

times confusing, but always fascinating topic of wine's cultural significance in the Roman World.

There are so many intriguing aspects about our past that, over the years, I have enjoyed writing on topics as diverse as Nigerian bronzes, Peruvian mummies, Chinese tomb goods, Etruscan wall-paintings, Renaissance terracotta sculptures, PreColumbian gold, and even medical aspects of the image on the Turin Shroud. My personal interests tend to be outside archaeology, however. I take constant pleasure from classical music—particularly Dvorak, Brahms, and Larssen—and learning about technical aspects of European painting. Despite the flavorsome topic of *VINUM*, however, my enduring hobby is the brewing of Belgian-style beers.

Stuart Fleming
June 16th, 2001

Art Flair
P.O. Box 323
Glen Mills, PA 19342-0323

Directors: Dr. Stuart Fleming and
          Dr. Gregory Maslow
Website for this book: www.artflair.net